Dizzy, Duke, The Count and Me

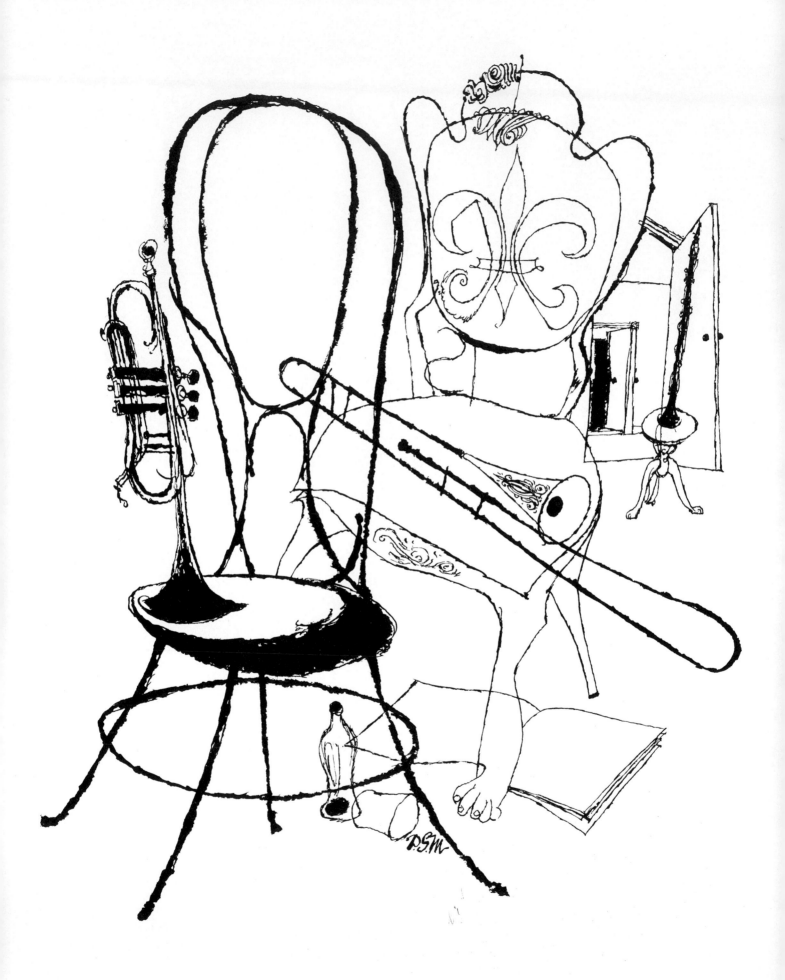

DIZZY,
DUKE,
THE COUNT and ME

The Story of the Monterey Jazz Festival

by Jimmy Lyons with Ira Kamin

Drawings by David Stone Martin

Photographs by Peter Breinig, Tom Copi, George Hall,
Jim Marshall, Veryl Oakland, Seymour Rosen, Grover Sales,
Jon Sievert, Bonnie Tiegel and Baron Wolman

A California Living Book

Acknowledgments

The Festival would never have happened if it hadn't been for a group of Monterey guys who supported my crazy idea for all these many years—the Jazz Festival Board of Directors. My thanks to the Executive Committee members—Hank Hutchins, President; Buck Bemis, Vice-president; Frank Wilkinson, Treasurer; Jimmy Costello, Secretary; and Doc Etienne, Director-at-Large. Frank, Mel Isenberger, George Wise and Sam Karas have been there since the beginning. My thanks too to Joe Turner, Bob Trenner, Judson Stull, Howard Brunn, Cleve Williams, Richard Eldred, and Ruth Fenton.

All the many great people who have been on the staff, serving with such devotion to the cause, certainly deserve my thanks. Needless to say, all the marvelous jazz artists I have met and known over the years, deserve my thanks as well. And those who I loved and admired and who left – Paul, Ralph, Duke, Louis and the rest – later!

Jimmy Lyons

Designed and produced by Adrian Wilson

Photocomposition by CBM Type

Photolithography and binding by Deseret Press

First Edition

Copyright © 1978
The San Francisco Examiner Division of The Hearst Corporation.
Special Projects, Suite 911, The Hearst Building, Third and Market Streets, San Francisco, California 94103.

Articles on pages 156-171 and on page 179 copyright © The San Francisco Chronicle.

Printed in the United States of America.

ISBN 0-89395-005-X (hardback)
ISBN 0-89395-006-8 (softback)

Library of Congress Catalog Card Number 78-052507 1/82

Contents

Dizzy Gillespie on stage at Monterey, 1977

Foreword

One of the great shining examples of the kind of association I have with Jimmy Lyons is the fact that contract-wise, our contracts never seem to catch up. I just assume that I'm playing the Monterey Jazz Festival. It's assumed that I'm going to be at Monterey every year.

Now sometimes that gets a little out of hand, such as last year, when I had the chance to play a theatre with Sarah Vaughan.

Now, I love Jimmy Lyons, but oh my God, Sarah Vaughan!

Monterey has a special meaning for me, because I understand that the people expect to see me there. My face is a part of the Monterey Jazz Festival just like that chair that they have. And at the end of the concert every year I start wondering what are they going to do next year? Because you can't top yourself all the time.

But over the years, the Monterey Jazz Festival has overextended itself—musically, I mean. Each year seems to be getting a little better. Sometimes it drops. Well, it can't be the same thing all the time. But it is the one festival where the musicians really feel a part of the festival itself.

At other festivals, you have a spot, you play the spot, you go wherever your spot is. But the Monterey Jazz Festival is unique in that the musicians feel they're part of what's happening, and that lends itself to a very high degree of creativity.

And the coup de grace was the hiring of John Lewis as musical director.

John Birks (Dizzy) Gillespie
(at Grace Cathedral, San Francisco;
October, 1977)

© Veryl Oakland

Jimmy Lyons and John Lewis, Monterey, 1977

Jimmy Lyons

Preface

There have been twenty Monterey Jazz Festivals, held every late September, in Monterey, California, since 1958.

It's Jimmy Lyons' Festival. He founded it and every year, with the help of his musical director, John Lewis, he puts the shows together.

I spent a few dozen hours with Jimmy Lyons over a couple of warm summer months, putting together this book about Lyons and the Festival.

He lives on Telegraph Hill in San Francisco in a small apartment with his wife, Laurel. He sits at a table by a window, smokes Camel cigarettes, bites the backs of both thumbnails and talks in the most listenable voice—he used to be a deejay, the first GI voice in Berlin—about the people who've passed his way the sixty years he's been on this earth.

The first part of this book is Jimmy Lyons' account of the Festival and parts of his life that led to the Festival. The second part is a more specific, chronological overview of the Festival's first twenty years.

I would like to express my special thanks to Dizzy Gillespie for doing the Foreword. When I talked to him about the book he was in the middle of a long road trip. He had an abscessed tooth and the insides of his face were hurting from that crazy way he has of playing the trumpet. He was incredibly gracious to all of us who wanted some of his time.

I would also like to thank Hal Silverman, Laurel Lyons, Tim Ware, Elaine Ratner, Ernie Beyl, Jean (Mrs. Ralph) Gleason, The Monterey Jazz Festival staff and Board of Directors, and of course Jimmy Lyons, for their great help and patience in putting this book together.

Ira Kamin
Mill Valley, May 1978

© Roberto Morrison

Jimmy and Laurel Lyons at the end of a Festival

Why a Jazz Festival?

by Ralph Gleason

The Monterey Jazz Festival—or any real festival, jazz or otherwise—can't be just a collection of concerts. It must be a thing unto itself, an entity beyond the individual performances, beyond the individual programs and greater than the sum of these.

The point of a festival is to be festive. To give and to receive joy and to present—in a jazz festival, at any rate—a wide diversification of styles and types of this music in as festive and benign a surrounding as possible.

To be successful as a festival, the grounds, the concerts, the musicians, the patrons and the atmosphere all have to jell together to be something more than one can find elsewhere. And this, of course, is what has happened these years at Monterey.

To be a true festival, there must be something for those who are not hard core jazz fans and who make this their sole jazz experience for the year. This, too, Monterey has provided.

The unusual combinations of musics, the special events, the virtuoso performances, but above all, the opportunity to see and to hear great artists in a great setting—that is the festival.

Seeing musicians as people has always been an attraction. "People out front don't know of the battle you wage back stage," Jon Hendricks wrote in his lyrics to Count Basie's "Blues Back Stage." At Monterey and at any true festival of music, the concert hall setting is avoided and the musicians make up part of the audience, walking through the grounds, rehearsing in the mornings and early evenings, themselves digging the festival. Charles Mingus was rehearsing well into the evening concert the night before his historic appearance in 1964 and latecomers lingered by the doors to hear him.

Ralph Gleason at Monterey, 1964

Not all the great music has always been on stage. There have been those delicious moments observed only by the people who came early or who stayed late and wandered around, such as the afternoon pianist Ralph Sutton rehearsed with Jimmy Rushing, the year that Ben Webster sat in on piano until Earl Hines arrived or the time Ben Webster was shooting pictures of the festival orchestra's saxophone section playing an arrangement of Ben's own solo on "Cottontail." These are the bonuses that make the festival worth more than anyone could dream of.

Of course, there's the opportunity to learn by listening to great artists from great eras in their own styles and settings. But that is only part of it. There are the once-in-a-lifetime performances.

Who could ever forget—who saw and heard it—the "Evolution of the Blues" with Jon Hendricks preaching and Jimmy Witherspoon and Big Miller singing and Miriam Makeba and Odetta and Pony Poindexter and the children gathered on-stage in a semi-circle around Jon?

Who could ever forget—who saw and heard it—Lambert-Hendricks-Bavan, dressed in monk's hoods and robes, singing in the cold night air behind Carmen McRae and Louis Armstrong in Dave and Iola Brubeck's "The Real Ambassadors." Or Lawrence Brown stepping forward to play "Poor Butterfly" or Duke Ellington's "Rockin' in Rhythm" or Bunny Briggs dancing "David Danced Before the Lord with All His Might" or Dizzy and Big Mama Willie Mae Thornton or Annie Ross, Jon Hendricks, Dave Lambert and Joe Williams ending the show singing with Count Basie?

Right from the very first night, when the unknown trumpet player sat in with Dizzy, Monterey has been this way and that's what makes a festival and that's why a festival is almost a necessity in this era of restraint and inhibition. For one weekend, anything goes and the results have been some of the greatest moments in jazz history.

The festival is for the musicians and the festival is for the patrons—both. Each one digs the other and they both dig the digging. A festival is to have fun, to be festive, to give and receive love. And love, like jazz, is a four letter word and surrounded these days with inhibitions and taboos. But at Monterey, for this one weekend, we are all free to love and jazz is free to be our music.

A festival is to have fun. You aren't *supposed* to like or dislike anything. You don't *have* to listen and you can come and go as you please. It's not a posh concert hall where silence must be preserved and it is only a tribute to the quality of the music and the musicians that silence has been granted (not preserved or enforced) during some of the great performances.

Nowhere in this country is there such a homogeneous gathering of people as at these festivals. Pass through those gates and leave behind all the traumas and the psycho dramas that inhibit the rest of the year. Glory in the music, in the people, in the place. Jazz is what you call it, everyone's his own expert (as is really true in every art form when you get down to it) and you pick your own likes and dislikes.

A jazz festival should be the best possible combination of enjoyments one can devise. Organization and improvisation, lyricism, strength, euphoria and the blues, individuals and groups, the scream, the cry and the whisper. It should all be there for you.

A festival, like music, is to be experienced. It is interesting, but not essential, to know things about the music and about the musicians. The music is enough by itself; so is the setting; so, too, are the people there. All together they make up one of the best things about living around here, even if it only happens once a year.

Reprinted from Monterey Jazz Festival Program, 1966

Jimmy Lyons

by Ralph Gleason

There are newspapermen, you know, who always seem to be where the news is. They don't need an assignment; some sixth sense leads, and wherever they go, that's where the news breaks.

In the field of jazz, Jimmy Lyons is like that. He has the ability and the luck to be there when there's jazz news in the making.

Back in the early '40s when Lyons, born in China the son of a missionary, was getting started as a disc jockey in Southern California, he heard the Stan Kenton band at Balboa Beach. Bells rang within Jimmy's head and he knew this was one of those moments. As the remote announcer on the Balboa broadcasts (that's his voice you hear on the Kenton Era discs) Lyons was in on the beginning of the great Kenton surge to success.

Later, after a stint in the Army, where he produced the "Jubilee" show for the AFRS on which Dizzy Gillespie, Milt Jackson, and Miles Davis were first presented on West Coast airwaves, he was in on the beginning of the Woody Herman "Four Brothers" band. For a year, Lyons was their advance man and sometimes they advanced so far they caught up to him—like the time they were all marooned in a snowdrift in Minnesota, stalled on the way to a one-nighter.

At the end of the '40s, Lyons settled in San Francisco, where his late night show, "Discapades," became familiar listening in fraternity houses, automobiles and homes on the Pacific Coast from Canada to Mexico.

On "Discapades," the listeners heard the first word about Dave Brubeck, Paul Desmond, Gerry Mulligan and Chet Baker and numerous other modern groups, as Lyons became a solo outpost for modern jazz. "The Lyon's Busy" and "Line for Lyons" by Brubeck and Mulligan, dedicated to Jimmy, have become jazz standards and a lasting tribute to his value in the music.

Today, as a resident of that classically beautiful coastal area, Big Sur, Lyons is devoting himself to the Monterey Jazz Festival and his winter series of "Jazz at Sunset" concerts (the hit LP "Concert by the Sea" by Errol Garner was recorded there) and to his Country Store in Big Sur. There's no truth in the rumor that he has a sign on the counter saying "Bebop Spoken Here," but if anyone goes inside to buy bread and ends up discussing Miles and Gerry and John Lewis, it won't be surprising.

Jazz musicians and fans alike owe a great debt to the handful of men like Jimmy Lyons who fought to keep this music on the airways. They could so easily have given up. So many did. But Lyons didn't and we are all the richer for it. Without him, there would have been no Monterey Jazz Festival.

Reprinted from Monterey Jazz Festival Program, 1958

Above left: Jimmy Lyons, age 2, with a cousin's milk goat

Above right: Jimmy, age 3, about to prove he can throw a ball as well left-handed as right

Left: Jimmy in the saddle, Cleveland Heights, Ohio

15

Jimmy Reminiscing

Dizzy and the Elephant

My father was a missionary for the Presbyterian Church in Peking, China, where I was born. He wasn't really a preaching minister, but he did his time with Billy Sunday, and I think having done time with Billy Sunday is what gave him his sense of pageantry. As far back as I can remember, in church, at Christmas time, there was always a pageant. You know, a little doll and the manger and the pretty girl who was Mother Mary. I once watched him do a pageant in downtown Cleveland that had a cast of thousands. I think it's the one thing I got from my father. I always want to do things grossly overdone. Like the elephants and Dizzy. I always wanted Dizzy Gillespie to appear unannounced at Monterey on the back of an elephant. Dizzy would do it, too.

Dizzy Gillespie is goofy, and everything everybody says about him is true. But he's also the best trumpet player alive. Besides, he's a very bright man; he isn't a clown. He's so articulate it's frightening. He plays the game that he can't be articulate. When I first interviewed him, I was on a San Francisco radio station. He would come by after his gig with a sandwich in a paper bag, and I'd ask him a question and all you'd hear would be Dizzy eating his sandwich.

Hot House

I was responsible for the Dizzy Gillespie-Charlie Parker quintet coming out to the West Coast in the '40s, when I was producing "Jubilee," the armed forces radio show.

They came through the back door of the studio. They were late. All the studio musicians were already up on risers on the stage. And we had a live audience, composed of injured guys from the hospital. Legs up in the air, casts, arms broken and all that. In they came—a little cat with a goatee and a chubby little alto saxophone player and the skinniest kid I ever saw, who is as skinny today as he was then, Milt Jackson, carrying a folded-up set of vibes. The bass player, another skinny kid, was Ray Brown. The piano player was Al Haig, and the drummer was a left-handed drummer, Stan Levy.

These kids came into the studio looking raggedy as you could possibly imagine. Dizzy turned and kicked off the first tune on the roster with his heel. "Hot House." The place went up in flames.

The studio guys just threw their instruments up in the air. They started laughing and holding onto themselves, watching these strange youngsters playing their funny music.

Jimmy Lyons broadcasting jazz in the '40s

Dizzy poses with his latest albums for Jimmy and cameraman Larry Russell

The Greatest Trumpet Player in the World

When my kids were very little, I introduced them to Dizzy Gillespie, with a preface that this is the greatest trumpet player in the world. Dizzy did his great thing with kids, kissed them and hugged them and shook their hands. They were very impressed.

The next year their grandmother took the boys from the Little League, with my daughter, to see a baseball game at Candlestick Park. Willie Mays hit his whatever thousandth home run.

When I asked them how the game was, I said, "You were certainly there at a great time. That was a big home run."

My daughter said, "You know something funny, daddy? He didn't stop to say hello when he was running around those bases."

I thought, "Of course, Dizzy Gillespie." He had overwhelmed them.

Dizzy Gillespie at a Festival rehearsal, 1961

Diz for President

Dizzy Gillespie was going to run for President of the United States. He had placards made, tee shirts. Everyone was marching around for Dizzy. He said he was going to live in the Black House and he was going to appoint Miles Davis as Secretary of State.

Then he made his announcement: "I have some information. I decided I will not run, very seriously; I don't have the time. I think I'm very qualified but I decided not to run."

The Contented Hour

I talked the army into letting me record the first Jazz at the Philharmonic that Norman Granz did in L.A. (Granz put on the show to raise money for the Sleepy Hollow Gang, a group of young Mexicans accused of raping a white woman.) I had Howard Duff as my announcer because he was in the service with me.

We used to do "The Contented Hour" out of Chicago and send it out to our guys overseas during World War II until Eisenhower sent a wire saying no one over here is contented; cut "The Contented Hour."

The Granz thing was part of a series called "One Night Stand." One of our guys would say, "And now from the beautiful Mirror Ballroom in downtown St. Louis . . ." We did it so the guys would scream if they were from St. Louis. They'd say, "Oh, boy, you should have seen me and that girl over in St. Louis." Actually the band was out of the Palladium. But it worked out very well.

Looking for Sergeant Lyons

I met Andre Previn when he was sixteen. I was doing the army radio "Jubilee" show. A little kid with high water pants walked into the studio in Los Angeles. I said, "If you're looking for the Safeway kiddie show, it's down the hall, kid."

"I don't belong there. I'm looking for Sergeant Lyons."

His father had been one of the great circuit judges in Berlin and a lot of the SS guys he had saved remembered him. So when the pogroms came, he was told by an SS trooper to be out of town by six in the morning or it's kaput in the ovens.

They stole away, taking nothing, getting to Brazil, and eventually to Hollywood.

Oscar Peterson

Norman Granz played me a record of a piano player he found. He came up to the studio when I was a deejay at KNBC in San Francisco. I couldn't believe it. I said, "This can't be possible."

"Oh, yes, it is. Wait. This guy's going to be one of the greats. I found him in Canada. His name is Oscar Peterson."

I worked out a deal with Norman for Oscar to come to Monterey. Oscar came and stormed the joint, like he always does.

On the Road for Woody

I came to San Francisco in 1948, after having been on the road with the Woody Herman band for one tour in '47. I was an advance man. I had been a disc jockey in San Diego and they hired me away. I was on all the radio stations in San Diego, and three in Tijuana. All on Sunday morning. All jazz and plugging cars.

I joined the Herman band in San Jose. Got out ahead of them and worked my way through San Francisco, across Idaho, down through Salt Lake; Scottsbluff, Nebraska; Evanston, Wyoming. Great towns. I'd call on the radio stations and take records to them. I took Dave Garroway two brand new boxes of "Bijou," by Bill Harris and the band. That was the big feature item on the old Columbia 78s.

Garroway was my personal idol at the time. He had the most listened-to jazz show in the country, out of Chicago, midnight till two. The best disc jockey I ever heard. He said all these oddball things, but he was very bright and always did marvelous shows.

The winter of '47 was the most atrocious winter I've ever seen. Driving through the midwest and Rockies. At the concerts, all the college kids yelled out "Near You," which was the big hit of the time. Woody would say, "What the heck is that?" He had a great band. They would jam that thing for 30 minutes. Herbie Stewart, Stan Getz, Serge Chaloff, Sonny Berman, Shorty Rogers, Earl Swope. Woody is the sweetest guy alive, and the best editor that ever lived.

Lots of Trees and Grass

About 1950 I met a guy named Gleason who I found out was at Columbia University the same time I was back in the '30s, when I was aspiring to be a young journalist. He introduced himself over the phone. He was then editing an insurance company house journal in San Francisco.

Ralph Gleason and I had some kind of instant rapport. I explained my ideas about wanting to do something like George Wein, after the George Wein thing had started in Newport. But before that even, in 1950, we discussed, wouldn't it be nice to have a sylvan setting with lots of trees and grass and all that and the best jazz people in the world playing on the same stage and having a whole weekend of just getting drowned in jazz?

So when I moved to Big Sur in '53, I called up Ralph and said, "I think I found it."

Twenty years ago the main function of Monterey was to service the army at Fort Ord. Other than that it was basically a fishing village, and it was a pretty sight. It had a little artist colony called Carmel, and Pacific Grove for the retired folks over in the pine trees where the fog sits heavily. And Seaside was springing up as a little town because a lot of the GIs had been there during training and when they got out of the service, they came back looking for a nirvana.

The more I thought about it, the more I thought it would be a perfect place to hold the kind of festival we had been talking about for six or seven years. Ralph Gleason, then the *Chronicle*'s jazz columnist, and I wanted to put jazz in a pretty place. We wanted it in the middle of a meadow, outside, in the wind, under the sky, where it belongs. So I started meeting with some Monterey business people.

When the Season Dies

Back then in Monterey, come Labor Day
the season died; it just fell right off the cliff.
What do you do for a town that only has the
overflow from the Bing Crosby Pebble Beach
golf tournament and the road races?

So my people and I went to various people
on the Chamber of Commerce and we made
our pitch. We called every interested party we
could think of, every doctor who had shown
some interest in jazz, every lawyer and all the
motel and restaurant owners. We held a
no-host luncheon down on the wharf. About
120 people showed up.

We promised a special event to be held
after the season dies, when the weather is still
good, so we could do it outdoors.

We formed the Monterey Jazz Festival,
Inc., which is a non-profit educational
corporation. Profits would be given to
musically oriented cultural events held on the
Monterey Peninsula. Period.

I sat with an artist for weeks and weeks
and weeks, a man named Coldie Whitman. I
said I would like to set up a chair of jazz at
the college there. He must have done a
thousand sketches until he finally got the
logo, which is the horn sitting on the
old-fashioned ice-cream-store chair. That to
me denoted the chair of jazz.

The Setting

Each jazz festival has its own identity.
We've been accused of bringing back the
same people every year, but we try to bring
in new faces.

Where we're lucky is in having the whole
thing in such a gentle area, a pretty area,
with trees and grass. The visual thing is as
important as the artists.

Billie Holiday

Keeping Billie Up

Billie Holiday played our first Festival. (She
died six months later.) She had no idea of
where she was or what she was doing. I
knew her condition, so I announced Gerry
Mulligan and Buddy De Franco. I told them
to stand very close to her, because she was
going out to center stage to sing.

Well, the people fell apart because it really
was Billie Holiday up there singing. She was
dressed in a kind of tight-fitting short skirt.
She was swaying from side to side. Buddy
De Franco would push her back and she
would lean the other way. And Gerry
Mulligan would gently push her back the
other way. The two of them kept her upright.

John Lewis

After that first Festival, Gleason came to me and said, "This was good. We got through it. Now let's go see John Lewis. I think it's time, because this first Festival was a shambles, although it came off. People enjoyed themselves, but we need some organization."

So I asked John Lewis, "Are you interested in doing it, because there's no money in it as far as I know?" He said, "Yes, what you have here is the germ of a great idea. But you must remember two things. European festivals are festivals and jazz is music. So be sure you always emphasize forevermore jazz and always festival."

John is always serious. That's his way. He was born in La Grange, Illinois, and was raised in Albuquerque. He graduated with a degree in anthropology in New Mexico. He went to music school in New York. (He teaches full time now—in New York.) He's the only Renaissance man I know.

When he feels titillated, he'll go have a martini with you. I've never heard him say goddamn.

Wein's Idea

Wein started three or four years before we did, at Newport, which is a lovely setting. All the kids got out of school in June. Then in July they'd get together in Newport. They'd put the beer in the back of the car and everybody'd come down and sleep on the beach and have a little beer bust and talk about "the great times we had in college." I think that was a great part of it.

Of course then the kids got a little rambunctious and started wandering the streets of this very quiet little resort town, Newport, and I think it had quite a bit to do with the eventual downfall of Newport. It attracted more and more and younger and younger. They expanded the facilities so the kids could camp out. Then some people came down and knocked over a five-foot snow fence and started tearing up chairs and hitting people over the head (1967).

Everybody in Monterey was wondering whether that might happen to us.

On with the Sweaters, Off with the Sweaters

I made an error one year and hired some friends of mine from the San Francisco Police Department. I was worried, because Wein was having problems in Newport.

I told them to help me spot any trouble in the audience. Because my theory is: jazz fans are lovers, they're not fighters. They're here to hear the music and have a great time.

I gave these friends of mine sweaters with a big S for Security.

Well, this one drunken guy got out of hand that year and my friends stomped him.

I said, "We can't have any of that. We'll have to call it quits."

They gave me back the sweaters and that was the end of that.

Gerry Mulligan (right) soloing with (left to right)
Mundell Lowe, Dizzy Gillespie, Illinois Jacquet, 1974

The Dreams

I have this recurring dream. What if I have a Festival this year and no one comes? I have dreams that bring all kinds of rain. And people are there who shouldn't be there. And I don't know who is there or why. It usually involves Gerry Mulligan.

One time (this is no dream) Mulligan arrived from Connecticut. "Well, I'm here."

"Well, I didn't hire you."

"Are you sure? I thought you hired me."

"No, I didn't hire you. Show me the contract."

He stayed and played the Festival anyway.

Come Back, Jimmy

We set up a fifteen-member Board of Directors for the Festival. They serve without pay; all they get is a meal the second Tuesday of every month when we have a business meeting.

I became their hired help. I quit the first year because I got mad at some people. I wasn't used to discussing things. Rationally. This was my baby and I didn't want to see anybody louse it up. The then president of the Board and another dear friend over the years came down to my store in Big Sur and said, "Don't worry about it. Come on back."

So I came back.

How Do You Do a Festival?

The first Festival, we had $6,700 to spend. We had asked people to loan us $100 each, on non-interest loans for a couple of years. We made a $1,000 profit that year. I didn't know how to do a festival. No one did. We muddled through. I went to my friends, Brubeck, Paul Desmond, The Modern Jazz Quartet, Dizzy, and asked them to come play.

The second year we had no money because we paid back the $6,700. When agents for artists saw we were serious about doing another Festival, they asked for fifty per cent of the money in advance. So we went to the guy who owned the biggest liquor store chain in Monterey County, because he cleaned up the first year, and asked him for a loan. He co-signed a $10,000 note.

Digging It

After the Festival that first year we found a pair of panties and a brassiere right near the seats.

We also found these two holes some guy had dug with his heels, you know, keeping time, and on each side of the hole an empty half-gallon wine bottle. He was with it all the way.

Two Piano Players

We don't give any 14-minute sets to anybody. We want the artists to play their jazz and do it in 35 minutes, which is about a set, maybe a little less than you normally have in a night club—unless you're meandering like the young avant gardists, then you want two hours to play one tune. Like Herbie Hancock in 1972. He started playing a tune, closed his eyes. Darlene Chan, my assistant, said, "I tell you Jimmy, he always closes his eyes and he doesn't look at a clock. So you'd better watch the time, because he's never gonna get out of this tune. He's gonna play three tunes? Forget it."

His 35 or 40 minutes came to an end. He was still on the same tune and I said, "Okay, I hate to do this. Start pulling the curtain slowly and stop at about eight feet and I'll talk to the guys on my end and tell them to pass the word along for Herbie to open his eyes. The goddamn thing's over with."

I walked out smiling graciously and all that, and I came off stage just as Herbie opened his eyes. He said, "What's happening? What's going on?" He looked like he'd just woken up. He was going to go on for another hour. He was probably upset, but he never mentioned it.

Another time McCoy Tyner's group was to open the show. His group was there four

Darlene Chan, Jimmy's right hand

through. I gave John the time sign and he said "No." He was having such a good time he didn't want to stop. So I started walking out there. He knew I was serious so he brought the thing to a close.

McCoy Tyner showed up at 8:45 or 9:15. I said "What happened?"

"My plane was late from Chicago."

"You should have called." I said, "If there's time, after Dizzy, if he gets done by midnight, you have a 25-minute set. And I'll honor the contract."

Dizzy came down at 12:15. We couldn't do it.

A Drummer's Blues

One year the Johnny Otis Blues Show was at Monterey. They had this young rock drummer. He had five women with him. He wanted to bring them on stage with him. The stage manager said, "No broads."

The kid said, "Wait a minute. I'm an artist. I've played Altamont, Woodstock . . ."

"Tell me the second annual Altamont, the second annual Woodstock."

hours early. They were all set up and ready to go. Right on time. I said, "Where's McCoy?"

"We don't know."

"You don't know?"

"No, we don't know."

I checked everyone. No one knew. I looked at John Lewis. I said "McCoy Tyner's supposed to open the show. He's not here."

He said, "Well, we're here." I had a house quartet (Lewis, Mundell Lowe, Richard Davis and Roy Burns).

We struck McCoy's group. I said "John, go out and play the blues." They sailed

27

The Repeaters

In the audience at Monterey we have little clusters of people, all been sitting next to each other for ten, fifteen, twenty years. All been sitting in the same seats. "You bring the pot, I'll bring the booze, and Joe'll bring the sandwiches."

One year we had a little rain and a friend of mine went out and bought long pieces of plastic and cut holes in them and sold places in the plastic where you could put your head up through it. Rows of people with plastic draped over them so they wouldn't get wet.

We had a couple who came every year, then they got divorced. The guy got the cabin in Tahoe and she got the front box at Monterey.

One guy died and left the box, in his will, to his wife. She and her son come down now.

The repeaters number nearly forty-two or forty-three hundred (out of seven thousand seats). They're buying into the locations where they'll still be sitting next to old Charlie, like last year.

Joining In

Two little old ladies who used to sit in front of some friends of ours, a few years back, would just get outraged by the people passing joints over them, and passing wine back and forth. They grimaced and carried on. About two years ago, they joined in and started taking the joints, taking the wine. Why fight it? They even passed some of their own.

Quarters

There's this guy who goes home every night in L.A. and puts all the quarters he's got in a jar to pay for his trip to Monterey. Every year he trades the quarters in for a check and sends it to us.

The Evening Before

Some chicks come down and solicit on the grounds; make their dates for later on.

One lady I know had a hotel down there. One year she had a big pimp and four or five chicks rent rooms. They took nice rooms. And they were busy all night long; big green Cadillacs driving up all night.

This lady said, "That was marvelous. They'd come down for breakfast and talk about the evening before, and I'd sit there and listen."

The Jazz Festival audience is part of the show

Looking for Watsonville

One year a delightful little gray-haired man came to Monterey. He said he was on his way to the Watsonville Fair. He represented a line of Italian sweaters and was doing one of his sales outings. He came to the Monterey Fairgrounds thinking it was the Watsonville Fairgrounds. So he bought a ticket and came to the show. He had such a great time he bought tickets to the rest of the Festival. On Saturday afternoon he bought a home in Carmel. He was an amateur painter on the side. He said, "I'd rather paint than sell." He was getting ready to retire anyway, so he retired to Carmel.

At a symposium we held at the college, after the Festival, someone said jazz brings a sad element to Monterey. I told them about this man, and he was there and told his story.

He had a painting show at a Carmel gallery. There on the wall was a Grandma Moses-type painting of an early Monterey Jazz Festival. It showed monks ice skating and playing trombones in front of the Carmel Mission, in front of a hill, with snow all over the hill. He gave it to me.

Dancing in the Aisle Time

Saturday afternoon is dancing in the aisle time. Seventeen minutes into the show, they start dancing. You can pull the curtain and turn a tape recorder on and they'd be dancing. It's usually started by a big white cat with a beard, stripped down to the waist, and a black lady with a big flowered hat. And then it's boogie in the aisles and the beat is always going.

In Touch with the Powers

There was a storm coming in one Sunday. It was supposed to come over Monterey at 9 p.m. The storm cloud came in the afternoon and that dumb cloud sat eleven miles off the coast and didn't move over Monterey until Monday morning.

Another time I woke up Sunday morning and it was raining cats and dogs. We started wiping off the seats with towels. Just before the concert I came out on stage and said, "I have an announcement to make. I've been in communication with a greater source and I've been informed that as soon as the curtains open, the rain will stop."

I opened the curtain. The rain stopped. I'll never try that one again.

Razorblade Toogaloo Shorty

I was looking for a blues artist for a show and I was on the phone with Alvin Baptiste, a friend who has the jazz program at Southern University in Baton Rouge. He said, "How about Razorblade Toogaloo Shorty?"

"With a name like that, already I'll buy him."

Alvin said, "Hold on, I'll put him on."

I never understood one word he said. At the end of our conversation, I said, "With a name like that, what do they call you for short?"

"They call me Blade, man."

He died three months later. A guy who had been looking for him for five years found him. Shot him full of holes. That's why I never had Razorblade Toogaloo Shorty.

Ornette Coleman and his white plastic sax, with Scott LaFaro on bass, 1960

The Elevator Operator

In 1959 John Lewis told me about an elevator operator in L.A. who played a white plastic alto saxophone.

"Come on, you gotta be out of your mind."

"No," John said. "There are things happening in jazz and a lot is going to be coming out of him."

It was Ornette Coleman. He played his can off at Monterey that year. Everyone's hair was on end.

My Kid Brother

Monk Montgomery is one of five kids. He kept telling me, "You should hear our brother. Oh, does he ever play guitar. Wait till you hear our brother. One day we're going to get him out of naptown" (Indianapolis). And they did. Wes Montgomery.

"Spoon" in Kentucky and Siam

Jimmy Witherspoon got his start at Monterey (1959). He was a blues singer who did well in this country and then went to Hong Kong after the war.

He was at some drinking dive in Kentucky, just across the border from Ohio. It was wide open; all the joints were pouring. He had been there for a couple of years.

I got his number, called him up and identified myself and told him about Monterey. He didn't have enough money to get out of town. He said he'd come if he had enough money to buy a used car and drive to L.A. I wired him $250 to buy himself a clunker and get out of that town.

One year, some time after that, we wanted him to play the Festival, but he said "The King of Siam called me. He's having a party and wants me to sing there." He couldn't make Monterey that year.

He was at Monterey in 1976, in a tux and gold medallion. Tore the place down. He sang that great song., "Don't Gotta Take You to the Dentist Tomorrow Babe Because I'm Gonna Knock Your Teeth Out Tonight."

Spoon became Ralph Gleason's favorite hugger. He always squeezed Gleason. Gleason, a diabetic, carried these chocolate bars in his pocket, and Spoon squeezed his candy bars into smithereens.

Cowboy

The closing of the Sunday night, the first year, was a Latin jam with Cal Tjader's group, with Mongo Santamaria and Willie Bobo. It was one of Cal's pinnacles, as far as groups. All of a sudden from out of nowhere a guy in a green suit walked up with a trumpet. We didn't know how he got on stage at all. He was in the middle of the stage playing his trumpet.

Later we found out he was some musician from San Francisco; his name was Cowboy. All dressed up in his green suit and he was gonna go out there and wail. He went out there and wailed till we got him off.

Same group, a few years later, Armando Perazza was playing congos. A guy came up from the front to the stage. Armando jumped up and started dancing and he danced the guy right off the stage.

Dancing and Announcing

I always liked big band music as a kid in high school in Southern California. I'd go to every appearance of every band I could get to, within reason. We were all dancers at the time. All us kids started a dance called the Balboa, which became popular. As a kid I hung around ballrooms all the time and danced with all the girls and met a lot of people.

I got a job in radio as an announcer in '39, in Santa Ana, at KVOE, "the voice of the orange empire."

At that time all the popular music was big bands. Glenn Miller and Tommy Dorsey and Duke Ellington and Count Basie.

A ballroom in Balboa Beach was auditioning bands; we were going to broadcast them live over the radio station.

Jimmy Witherspoon singing the blues, 1960

This was in the spring of '41. One bandleader was named Harry Wam and I don't even know what happened to him. The other band was led by a big tall gangly kid named Stan Kenton. I told the owner of the ballroom that this was the best band to hire for the summer. So he hired the Kenton band. The first broadcast was July 3, 1941.

The music reflected the kids who were all being drafted at that time. Everything was upset. So the band had an upset sound. The staccato sound of the early Kenton band fit the mood of the time. You could dance to it too.

I was dancing to the Kenton band all the time. I decided I had gotten to be a big man; I was all of 23. So I got married to a little girl who was the best dancer of all. We hung around the Kenton band and we were very close to Kenton. She and I sat with him in a bar in Balboa Beach to wait for the birth of his first daughter.

After his exposure in Balboa Beach, Kenton went to the Palladium in L.A., which of course was a marvelous experience for him; that was the big time.

He and I walked down the street one night, on Vine, and there was a huge billboard, said "Stan Kenton" in green with fire shooting out of all the letters—"Now at the Palladium." I asked him, "What does that mean to you?"

And he said, "I'm just selling my potatoes."

The Kids Come Back, Grown

Kenton always had an eagerness to bring young people into the band, brilliant young people who can do compositional work and arrangements.

Just today a kid called me who's arranged a Chick Corea thing, "Celebration Suite," for Kenton.

His name's Alan Yankee. He came from a school up in Oregon. McMinnville High School. One year I judged a choral thing up there, at Mt. Hood College in Portland. When these kids came on and sang and won the whole thing I said, "Wow, this is something we never had." I offered them $500 to appear on my stage. And the kid who did all the arrangements was Alan Yankee. It's amazing how it works out.

A Fill In

Once I was stuck with the Kenton band without Kenton. He was ill. Stars are very important. The trumpet player looked like a banker leading the band.

Knowing full well Kenton wasn't going to be there I called Willard Alexander, who's always represented big bands including Basie for the last 30 or so years. "I've got to have some help."

Willard: "I'll tell you what. I'll call around."

He called back. "Buddy Rich broke his foot chasing his daughter around the pool in Palm Springs. He's recuperating. He'd like to test out his foot. He'll come up if you give him a suite and pay his passage and have a limo pick him up at the San Francisco airport."

"What else?"

"Nothing. Buddy's offering to do this."

Then we had a star, right, to go with all those wonderful spear carriers.

Buddy Rich

The great thing about Buddy's band is they don't know what they're gonna play. He just hollers a number and they go fumbling through the book. The band he has now is the best band he's ever had. Most of them are out of North Texas State. The average age is 23, 24. Marvelous trumpet section. They play all these tunes written 100 years before they were born. I just heard them do an old tune popularized by Matt Dennis called "The Folks Who Live on the Hill." I listened to it. I hadn't heard it in twenty years and I cried.

Buddy Rich, 1973

Perfectly Basie

I danced to Basie in the '30s, met him in the '30s, used him in the army shows in the '40s. I've been a Basie fan all my life, as anybody who's interested in jazz should be.

He's not a very communicative guy. I saw him last year at the Orange County festival and I said, "Hi, Base, how are you?"

And he said, in that low voice he puts on, "Fine, James, fine."

I said to him one year, "I want you to come to Monterey and I want to recreate the Kansas City Seven. Is that okay?"

"Whatever you say, James."

"Thank you, that's all I need."

"Perfectly okay."

Plink Plink

Basie was supposed to be there in '76 but had a heart attack on me. (He recuperated and was one of the hits of the '77 Festival.) The band played well—it always does—but you miss that plink plink. Ain't the same without that lovely little round man.

Helen, Between Retirements

Helen Humes first appeared in Monterey in 1962. We decided it was time to bring her back. She was on the verge of not singing anymore. Her folks were getting old and living in Lexington, Kentucky; so she went back to kind of take care of them. She took off for eight or nine years. She went to work in a munitions factory down there. I said, "Why don't you come out and sing for us?" And she did.

The Real Ambassadors

Dave Brubeck had written a thing called "The Real Ambassadors." His wife, Oly, was the narrator. It was to include Louis Armstrong, Carmen MacRae, Lambert, Hendricks and Ross. It was supposed to go on Broadway; never got there.

Dave was worried about Louis' eyesight; he was worried that Louis would have a hard time remembering the words. Dave went up to Louis' hotel room before the performance at Monterey and there in a darkened hotel room, at two o'clock in the morning, Louis sang all the lyrics. He had memorized them. "So don't be worried," he told Dave.

"The Real Ambassadors" was about an American jazz musician going off to Africa. All those black and white games come up.

There's a part in the narrative where the real ambassador flies into Africa. He has to fly into the hinterlands on a small plane.

Just when they got to this part in the story, a small plane, without radio, flew over the Monterey Fairgrounds. It was the most hair-setting-on-end thing I've ever seen in my life. The guy up there had no idea what he was doing and we had no way of getting him out of there. A dumb little plane flying over, just at the right moment.

Two Souls

Dave Brubeck and Paul Desmond wouldn't talk all day; each would be leading his own life. When they got on stage at night they would talk to each other with their instruments. They would tell each other where they'd been all day with quotes from old tunes. They had kind of a hard friendship to figure out; well, they were like two souls.

Paul Desmond and Dave Brubeck playing with the Jazz Festival Orchestra, 1958

Whose Key?

Monk had done a recording thing at Carnegie Hall with a rather big group behind him. I had Buddy Collette, who grew up with Monk, take the record, arrange the music from the record.

Monk flew in to Monterey that year. We picked him up; we picked Nellie up (Monk's wife). Took him to the rehearsal hall where Buddy was all set—he had been running the guys through it all day. Monk walked in, sat down at the piano, said "Are you ready?"

Buddy said, "Yes, we're ready. Let's get going."

They started playing. Monk stopped them. "Wait a minute, wait a minute. It's in the wrong key."

Buddy said, "It's your tune. I took it from the record. It's not the wrong key, it's your key."

"Oh, did I write it that way? Well, I guess I really didn't know what key I wrote it in."

Monk gets into his mysterious ways. It came off very well. Everyone had been waiting to see Monk at the Festival. He still had his overcoat on. He got up during one of the numbers, went behind the piano and did his little dancing, came back and played some more.

Thelonious Monk arriving at the 1964 Festival

Pals—Thelonious Monk, Dizzy Gillespie, Gerald Wilson, 1963

Mingus

1964 was the first year I had Charlie Mingus at Monterey. I've known him since he was seventeen years old, playing after hours in L.A. I was in the army then and I would join my friends and watch this funny chubby bass player. This kid was playing "Body and Soul," standing on a little table, playing his bass, playing absolutely marvelously.

I used him a lot on the army shows. Mingus was dying to meet Oscar Pettiford, who was playing bass with Duke Ellington. He wanted to take lessons. After they met, Pettiford stood back and said, "Look, kid, you don't need lessons from me. You better stop cutting in on my neighborhood. You're too good for me to give lessons to."

When his group (with Red Norvo and Tal Farlow) kind of disbanded, Mingus would come by my San Francisco radio show. Two in the morning, I'd find this huge figure of a man huddled up in a coat, with the wind blowing down Taylor Street like you wouldn't believe. He'd look pretty down in the dumps, so I'd give him a couple of bucks. Then he went to L.A., got a name, and went to New York.

At Monterey, he came up with Dannie Richmond on drums. He came on that stage ready for bear. He handed me a bill on the back of an envelope, for portage and for cab fare. He played the most magnificent set I've heard in my life. He played piano; did some Duke tributes. I tell you I went straight up in the air.

The following year we brought him back. But there was a screw-up with some records he recorded himself and wanted to sell at Monterey. You had to buy them through him. He said the records were never shipped out here. That's when I had to get on my knees.

He was wearing a bowler hat, dark suit. He got me on stage and said to his band, "I think I'll just take the money and pay you guys off and this ofay bastard is standing here and he's going to make me play when he hasn't done what he was supposed to be doing." He looked at me and said, "You want me to play?"

I said, "Of course, it's in your contract. I've given you half the money."

"Okay, you get down on your hands and knees and beg me."

I got down on my knees.

He did two tunes and marched off to the Saints ("When the Saints Go Marching In").

The Monday after the Festival my wife Laurel and I went down to Big Sur for dinner with some friends. Who walks in but Mingus with some guy from the language school.

Well, we were there, and I felt a little better, and I sent a drink over. He said he'd accept the drink and sit with us a while. We were staying at the campground. We invited

Jazz in the sunshine–the view from the stage, 1964

him to stay with us. He said, "I'd sure like to stay down here. I've never been in the country in my life."

He told the guy driving him, "I'm gonna stay here." He had a U.C.L.A. date the next Friday. He had nothing with him, just the clothes he was wearing. Next morning he showed up in his jeans, and strapped to his belt were two hunting knives in sheaths. And he had a scarf around his head.

He suggested we have crayfish for dinner, said he'd go down and catch them. When he got down in the water, he slipped and fell.

He yelled, "Grab my arm, grab my arm!" He had one of those $2,000 watches on. We grabbed the watch.

We had crayfish and salad and some booze. We ate by the fire. We kept eating and eating.

The outdoors intrigued him. The big trees. He forgot all about his gig in L.A. He blamed everyone for not telling him. I had to haul him in a little VW to the airport.

The Teagardens: (left to right) Jack, Mom, Norma, Charlie, 1963

The Family

Jack Teagarden (trombone) came out in 1963 with his brother Charlie (trumpet). And they had Norma, who lives here in San Francisco, playing piano. And then Jack Teagarden introduced his mother, who taught them all; she was in the audience. We brought her up from the audience, and she jammed with Charlie and Jack and Norma. Jack died six months later. It was one of those crazy things, where the whole place welled up. The whole place was awash with tears, of joy, you know.

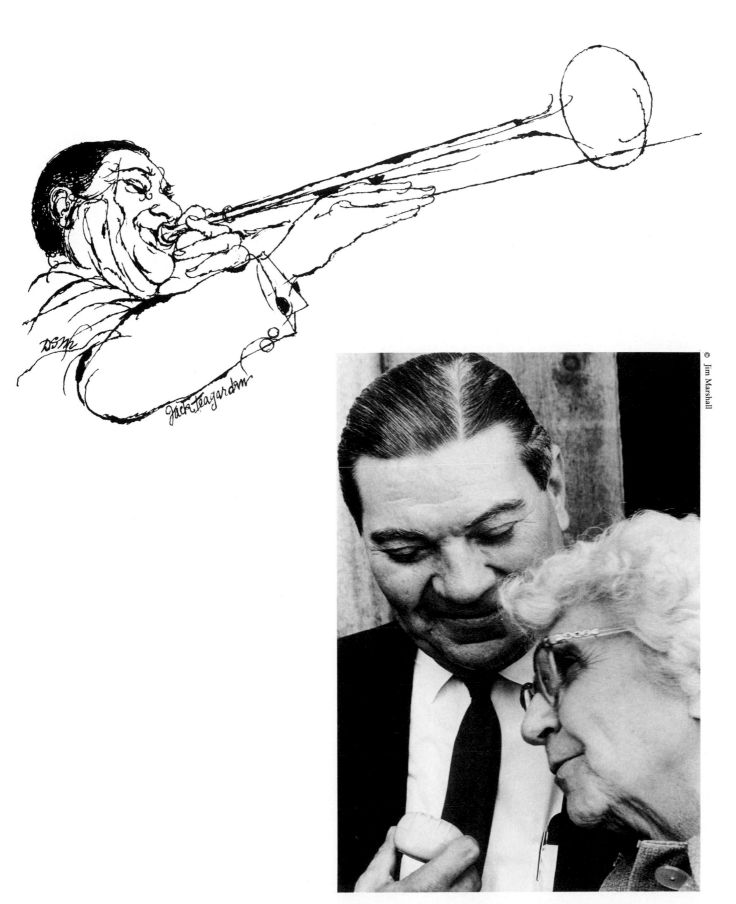

Jack Teagarden and Mom, Monterey, 1963

Lost Ticket

Bill Evans came out to play from Miami. He had his wife with him. He screwed me out of a plane ticket.

What happened was they said they had messed up or something and I said, well come on ahead anyway. Get on the plane and get out here. He had his wife with him and no ticket. I said, "Buy one."

He never paid me back.

Two years ago when I hired him, I took it out of his pay. He realized what he'd done.

He never ceases to amaze me. He doesn't look like he could play that well or understandingly. And he's so damn good!

Mrs. Smith

In 1966, someone came back to the office at the Festival and said, "There's a Mrs. Smith in the front office to see you."

"There's a million Mrs. Smiths. Which one?"

It turned out to be Fischella Smith, Willie Smith's widow. He was Lunceford's great little alto saxophone player. She's now running a home for wayward children in L.A. When I got out of the army and had no place to go I lived with them for two weeks. They took me in and treated me like a son. She came back into the office and we had a drink to Willie. You make good friends along the way, and they just pass on, seemingly in droves.

Which Part Do You Wanna Hear?

Ten years ago we opened with an evening of Mel Torme. I knew him when he was a boy drummer, when he was dropped in L.A. by the Chico Marx band. He came out of Chicago with the Chico Marx band, playing drums.

He introduced himself to me as a singer when I was doing Armed Forces radio. He wanted to get some copies of some of the things I had done with Duke Ellington, at various dances.

I said, "You know the Ellington music?"

He said, "What tune you want to hear?"

He sang everybody's horn part to me. I said, "Uh oh, look out."

The Tenth

We had gotten through nine years. This was the tenth year, 1967. We wanted to have all these geegaws, make it a celebration. NET filmed it. We set out all these helium-filled balloons, while Don Ellis played an overture. He was doing one of those crazy 32/8 things. We had gold coins; threw them out to the audience. We'd invited a group of Europeans; we were trying to internationalize ourselves. We had Jean Luc Ponty and George Grunz and Sven Asmussen and Nils-Henning Orsted Pederson: the international set.

We had Big Brother and The Holding Company with Janis Joplin. She was prancing around backstage the whole time: "We got to get out there and get 'em."

We had Ornette Coleman back and Dizzy and Earl Fatha Hines and Carmen McRae. That was the year Dizzy came out while she was singing. He came out very quietly behind her and told everyone to hush up. She was singing one of those lovely Sarah Vaughan things. And Dizzy started doing these little obligato things. She grabbed the mike: "Oh, my God, no." She swung at his ass, goodnaturedly. Then he sat on the lip of the stage with his legs crossed the rest of the set, with his horn parked right in front of him, in the dark.

Double Dudley

John Handy is a sweet guy, out of Dallas. He was trying to be a boxer at one time. He wore these funny little hats. He plays marvelous alto. We traveled on a college circuit together once. We were driving late at night and Handy said "Uh oh, a double dudley."

"What's that?"

"Well a dudley is a cop. Two of them is a double dudley."

(Ernie Beyl, Jimmy Lyons' publicist for the last 15 years, tells this story about Jimmy and John Handy: "John Handy had been playing in New York with Mingus, but his career was at kind of a lull. He was playing the Both And, a club in San Francisco. Ralph Gleason called and said, 'Has Jimmy heard John?' So we went. The group was 20 minutes into this tune, 'Spanish Lady.' It was wild, really going. Handy looked up from the stand, saw us walk in, and stopped. We got seated. And when Jimmy was seated, whap, he started 'Spanish Lady' from the beginning. When he ended the set, Handy came over and sat down at the table. And Jimmy said, 'Okay, okay, you're at the Festival.'")

John Handy, 1965

The Tipalet Experience

1969 was the Tipalet experience. The Tipalet people from Muriel cigars underwrote some of the shows. They passed out these cigars at the door. They came in blueberry, cherry and strawberry flavors. You couldn't hardly see through the haze. Everyone was lighting up these terrible things. I'll never forget that year no matter what happens, never forget that scent.

The Tipalet people were not all that excited afterwards. There were lots of cigars left over.

Sly

We decided to hire an act that'd draw younger people. 1969. Sly and The Family Stone.

The roadies all came in. About fifteen of them. Brought in these huge speakers, 8 feet high.

Sly came out screaming because someone forgot his private stool that he always had to use, had to be sitting right up there. He went into this long, long thing, screaming and hollering at his people. He stood up and walked out and into the dressing room.

I said, "Someone get him a substitute stool and I'll go down and see Sly."

I said, "Look, Sylvester, you been in radio, I've been in radio. I'm putting on a show; you're an artist. Come on, please, just for old times sake, for old radio guys." I said, "I can't hold up the show any longer." There was about a 25-minute wait and the natives were getting restless.

Whatever I said finally worked. He went out and played.

A Ferrari in Monterey

I have known Miles Davis since he was seventeen years old, back in '46 or '45, I guess, when he was playing third trumpet with Benny Carter's band. I bought him his first drink. There was a party for Duke Ellington out in Beverly Hills and Oscar Pettiford and I were the bartenders. Okay. So Oscar and I gave this kid a drink, the first drink he'd ever had, he says.

In the ensuing years I got to know Miles very well. I became very fond of the way he played and very fond of the guy, in spite of his irascibility. Miles was Miles. He came from a well-to-do family in St. Louis, a dentist's son or a doctor's son. He had a very good life. Miles, if you will, was a spoiled kid. But he was a good player and I loved the way he played. When Bird came through St. Louis he heard this kid play and he said, "You better leave town, kid, because you play too good to stick around here."

So the years went by. Pretty soon Miles played the old Blackhawk out here. For five years I said, "Miles, come play for me."

"Oh, who wants to play any dumb old festival? I can play any festival I want."

"Miles, come play mine. You're my friend."

"No, I'm gonna be in France. Can't do it."

One time I said, "Come on, come down to Monterey. It's beautiful country. You've never been there, you've never taken time off to relax a little bit. You're a New York kid. Don't sit around and fight with Columbia and have them buy you more apartment buildings in New York City to pay you off. You'll enjoy the sunshine."

He looked at me and said, "You need the sunshine more than me."

Next year he came back to Blackhawk. We were standing outside. He said to me in that

Miles Davis plays Monterey, 1964

gravelly voice, "When's that damn festival?"

"September. I've been asking you for five years. You wanna play?"

"I don't know. Maybe I wanna play it. I'll call you."

Miles called. He said, "I'll play it."

So Miles flew down to Monterey. It was in 1962. He called New York and had them fly his Ferrari out. He had the time of his life, hanging out with everybody. He came out and played a marvelous set. Later he came roaring up from the bar. He had been hanging out with Dizzy and Harry James. I said to him, "You want me to give the money to Benny (Benny Shapiro, his manager at the time)?"

"No, give it to me. I need it."

So I gave him $2,500 in cash. My wife was standing there and Miles took the money, folded it up and shoved it down her bosom. "Keep it for me; I'll pick it up later."

He came back at three in the morning, looking for his money. He thought he'd lost it.

That was Friday night. He hung around for the whole Festival. On Sunday night, Dizzy walked out on stage without a trumpet. I didn't know what had happened. Then Harry James and Miles Davis walked out with a pillow and handed Dizzy his trumpet on the pillow: Harry and Miles bringing out the master's trumpet.

Something New

In 1969 John Lewis told me, "Miles has been to my house every night for a week. He said he hasn't found himself and he wants to try something new at Monterey."

This was the night he went out and played and he got boos from the audience. He knows my audience. I know my audience. Miles was playing all these squibbling things, out of which came "Bitches Brew" and other things.

I told John, "I don't understand it."

Miles found out this was the way he wanted to go. People ask me, "What's new in jazz?" I say, "The way Miles plays tonight, any night."

He has the most creative mind for that horn. Miles was terribly disappointed that night at Monterey. But he's got to find his own way and he's got all the money in the world, and he owns half of New York and that was what he wanted to do. And I said to Miles, "Go ahead. You always bring out new kids who turn out to be monsters anyway." Like Jack de Johnette, Chick Corea, Wayne Shorter, Dave Holland, and so on.

Big Names

Steve McQueen came to Monterey because he wanted to hear Miles Davis, because he's a Miles Davis fan. Well, McQueen called me and said, "Would it be all right if I came in to hear Miles Davis?" I said, "No problem, just show up and I'll get you in." Miles Davis turned out to be the biggest Steve McQueen fan going.

Wilt Chamberlain was a jazz fan. Freddie Williamson, a big jazz fan. Kim Novak. Merv Griffin showed up. Clint Eastwood wore a mustache and funny dark hat, incognito style. Come to enjoy the jazz.

A Big Bump

Bobby Blue Bland, God was he good. When he came out, the whole audience started doing the bump together. 7,000 people. One total sensuous sway.

The Jazz Rose

1971 was the year of the roses. Some guy called me one day from a nursery in Ontario, California, and wondered what it would be like to tie in a rose with a jazz festival.

They had a new rose that they had just come up with. They thought they'd name it "Jazz Fest" and could they tie it in?

They sent 500 plants in bloom. There were plants all over the fairground; we lined them up in front of the stage, two tiers deep from the lip; solid banks of roses. It was the silent star of the Festival. The Jazz Fest rose; it was marvelous. I'd like to work it out again.

Dizzy and Louis

1971 was the year we dedicated to Louis Armstrong. Dizzy adored Louis.

When Dizzy first started out, Louis castigated all those young Turks like Dizzy and Charlie Parker. They came out of a different school. I dare say it was an age thing. The way I castigate younger artists today, who will be monsters ten years from now.

But Louis was a sweet, gracious man. I have letters from him here. He always signed them, "Red beans and rice-ly yours."

Little Summer Dresses

The high school choir from McMinnville came in '71. They sang in churches on the way down from Oregon. All these kids came down in a school bus; they worked out a deal to stay some place in Monterey. We started rehearsing. And I said, "I want you to learn the parts behind Carmen McRae's solo on this record." So they studied it and they had it worked out. And they stood on risers they brought with them on the bus.

I saw Carmen and asked her if she was ready to rehearse these kids. So they ran it down a couple of times, just she and the piano player to get her part straight. "Are you ready, kids?" she said.

"Oh yeah."

She started to sing and they came in and she just turned around and stopped everyone and said, "Wait a minute. What are we rehearsing for?"

And the kids all giggled.

She said, "Oh, my God, that's beautiful, better than the professionals."

That afternoon they came on stage. All the girls came out in summer print dresses; each one came out with a rose and handed it to Carmen.

They got me backstage and said, "We'd like to thank you, Mr. Lyons."

"Well, you were just marvelous."

One of them reached behind his back and pulled out a myrtlewood tray; in the center was a plaque to me and the Jazz Festival, from the McMinnville Twilighters, or whatever they called themselves, and I burst out bawling.

Keith Squyres, baritone sax, California All-Star High School Jazz Band, 1977.

Kids

Slowly, the high school band concert on Sunday afternoon has become my favorite part of the entire weekend. You look out there and see a kid who'll come up and say, "Hi, I want to thank you for the wonderful time I've had playing at Monterey." It makes it all worth it.

I meet these kids, years later, all the time. It's inspiring for me. Patrice Rushen started off in a high school band with us. Mary Fettig played with a band; two years later she joined the Kenton band.

Once there was this six-foot-tall kid, teeth in braces, playing guitar. Glenn Jeffries. Mundell Lowe was really impressed with his playing. He told him, "If you're really interested in guitar, you come up to the mountain. When you're on your way to the peak, you stop at a couple of caves along the way, but you want to get to the peak. I'm going to arrange for you to take private lessons with John Collins, who was Nat Cole's old guitar player."

The kid went to study, then turned left on us all and went to study to be a computer operator. Now he wants to play again.

Hoofers

Someone said, "Why don't you get some tap dancers?" So in 1973 we got Baby Lawrence, John T. McPhee, Buster Brown and Chuck Green. They were wonderful. They beat me out of $400 in hotel room bills and rented cars. And I didn't care.

A Father and Daughter

We had Jimmy (father) and Stacy (daughter) Rowles in 1973. Stacy was 17 and she had made the all-star band, playing trumpet and flügelhorn.

She came up and said Jimmy wasn't in good shape, but she would go over to his hotel every hour on the hour and check on him until the Sunday night when they appeared. She was worn out, worn to a frazzle. She wanted to make sure her old man was going to play well.

I know he's in good condition now and working and doing very well in New York.

Paul Desmond used to talk about going down to hear Jimmy play in a club in New York and challenging him to play old tunes. They'd play that game all night.

In Memoriam

One thing comes back to me very vividly about Paul Desmond. Back when I first met him I was on the air in San Francisco and I was asked, I think by Dave Brubeck's wife Oly, if I could emcee a show with the Dave Brubeck octet in the Marine Memorial Theatre. That led to my knowledge of the Brubeck thing.

I was on the air from midnight to two then, and I started getting calls from one of the kids I met at the octet concert. The alto saxophone player. He would say, "Is it possible to come up to the radio station?" And I'd say, "Sure, why don't you come up?"

Well, this went on for seven, ten days, and I finally said, "Look, son, just come on up. Here's how you come up the front door of the building. Just the engineer and I are here now. I'll buzz the buzzer and he'll come down and let you in. It's no problem. I'd like to have some company." He said, "Okay, I'm at the Oakland end of the bridge. I've crossed the bridge three times back and forth trying to get the nerve to call you and to come up."

He came up, and from then on I became his surrogate father. I guess his father had died by then; his father was a copyist with the symphony.

The first dog we had down in Big Sur we named Desmond. He ran away eventually, ran off with some woodcutters.

Note:

(In August 1977, true to Paul Desmond's request, Jimmy Lyons threw Desmond's ashes over Big Sur. He scattered them from a small airplane. He had a martini at his feet, toasted Paul, and threw the martini out the window too. Glass, olive, toothpick went down. Only the liquid splashed back in Jimmy's face. Paul Desmond loved martinis.

When Jimmy Lyons and I were getting together once, twice a week, doing this book, people started dropping. Paul Desmond died on Memorial Day. When he died he looked older than Jimmy Lyons.

A week before, Stan Kenton fell in a parking lot in Reading, Pennsylvania, and fractured his skull. Jimmy Lyons met his first wife, Audree, dancing to Kenton.

Woody Herman was recuperating from a bad car crash. Jimmy and Woody would hang out in hotel rooms, years ago, and Woody would pad around the room in his socks and grab a scotch. Years later he switched to beer, because Woody would be driving and he wouldn't want to drive drunk.)

I.K.

The end of a hot set, 1970. Left to right: Duke Ellington, Joe Williams, Woody Herman, Paul Gonsalves, Joe Benjamin, Harold Ashby

Mr. Ellington

1974 was dedicated to a gentleman named Mr. Ellington.

That was the year a Fuji bank guy called me. He said, "Why don't you bring a Japanese band to Monterey." He said The New Herd was the best band around.

"I can't afford to bring a whole band from Japan."

He said, "I can help you. I can get the government to help pay."

So I paid the rooms and they paid transportation.

None spoke English. They wore these happy coats. I looked up when they were on stage. I could have sworn there were only five trumpet players.

I was right. The sixth was Dizzy.

Duke's Charms

Duke Ellington had his grandma groupies. He attracted them at twelve and eighty-five. Dressed to kill. Made up like, you know, it was Christmas night. Came back to see their idol. Beehives and blue hair. He would kiss their hands. He would wear you out with all that.

He was a great put-on artist. He used to travel with this doctor's kit. He'd open it up and say, "James, are your ankles all right? Are your feet all right?" He had yellow pills, blue pills. If you had bursitis in your left elbow, he had different color pills for it.

He gave me a belt once, in some little club in North Beach. He said, "Reach in there." He had a bunch of cloth belts. "Pick one. Take it home." It was about fourteen miles long. Looped around twice.

Once he drafted a piece of music in the basement of the Paramount, based on ladies' phone numbers he knew. Neither of us, Ralph Gleason or I, had the foresight to rip it off. It was just a piece of paper on top of a shelf. I guess it sat there for months. It was just a piece of something, but it was Duke's.

James, Love

One time I got a call from Duke Ellington at three in the morning. "James, love," in that unmistakable voice.

"Yes, maestro?"

"James, love, I have a request to make of you. I need to have a favor from you. It won't cost you very much money. Can you bring $500 more (for Duke's upcoming concert at Monterey), because I want to bring a dancer out for Grace Cathedral. I will repay you. I want Bunny Briggs to do the Dance to the Lord (for Duke's sacred concert at Grace)."

The next year he brought Bunny Briggs with him to Monterey. No charge. "I brought you a present," he said.

Who's Calling?

The crowd always goes up when Clark Terry comes out. He knocked everyone out one year when he came out with his suit coat back on his shoulders and played "Killer Joe" like a street corner cat.

Last year (1976) I had to fight him to go on with Cal Tjader and Luis Gasca, another trumpet player.

Clark said, "I'd feel a draft if I went out there. The guy'd hate me!"

I said, "Go on, Clark, Luis would fall over if you came out and played with him. He'd love it playing next to a hero."

Afterwards, Luis thanked me for having Clark jam with them.

Clark called me the other day. He went into this long deep-south-field-nigger voice. I realized who it was after the first two minutes. But the first minute I was really upset. I didn't know who it was. He said, "James, I want to ask one question. Am I invited to come to Monterey this year or do I have to pay my own way?"

"You're invited."

"Okay."

Clark Terry and Sarah Vaughan, 1971

Night Wails

In '75, the Thursday before the Festival, Mundell Lowe married Betty Bennett at Monterey. The judge who was president of the Festival married them. We had a little party; the ceremony was performed. And out of that cold night, fog, getting hazy, we heard the most beautiful music ringing out. It was Clark, playing "When I Fall in Love."

Ready To Play

We had the Olympia Brass Band in '76. I thought Delta or the City of New Orleans would fly them out, but they didn't. I got stuck for all the transportation. But they were such sweet, mellow guys. They played one tune and split, before every show. We'd send them down to the grounds through the side gate. They'd be there an hour-and-a-half in front of the concert, toodling around, ready to play. "Stop them, for God sakes. The show doesn't go on for half an hour." But you can't stop them. They had 700 people dancing with them whenever they played.

Sarah

I once got into a situation I had never been in in my life. The crowd wouldn't quit. They wanted to have more, more, more of Sarah Vaughan. She came backstage and said, "What am I gonna do?"

I said, "You made a recording about four years ago of the Lord's Prayer. Run out and sing The Lord's Prayer. And before they know whether to applaud or pray, we'll close the curtain." And it worked. It was gorgeous. It was an old Musicraft single. I remember it from playing it on the air all the time.

Call It Music

Our audience got tired of that African-percussion-crossing-field-holler-spiritual-street-band-ragtime-blues-boogie-woogie-swing-bebop-samba-ballad-R&B-avant-garde thing. I think people got tired of that historical crap. They know it now. They just want to hear good music.

The Youngers and the Warriors

I'm not George Wein or Bill Graham. I'm not making a fortune off Monterey. I love that dumb Festival because it's mine. I thought it up. Ralph helped me, and so did some good guys from Monterey way back then. We made it happen. We got through the grizzly first years and it's become a rather prestigious Festival (The American Salzberg, it's been dubbed.) We do no big push job, no big commercial thing. We're trying to younger it out a little bit, but in 1977 we had all the old warriors and there ain't many of them left. We brought back a lot of warriors just before they died. We've been responsible for bringing back a lot of people whose careers had fallen apart. You feel good about that. You can fault me. But you can never please everyone. Next year I'm going to put out more money and bring out some of these young jazz artists. We'll see how it goes.

The Critics—The Defender

Over the recent years we get more and more criticism for being conservative, for having the same people back every year, for not bringing the new jazz players.

I keep thinking of John Handy's comment about Monterey. "Don't criticize it for what it's not. Don't forget what it is."

The Festival Years

Lambert Hendricks and Ross

1958

Monterey was scared to death. The very idea: bringing jazz to a respectable community. George Wein began that kind of craziness four years earlier in Newport, Rhode Island. The results were still not in. When you take music that's been played in clubs for fifty-some years and you stick it in the middle of gentility and wind, you run the risk of either ruining the gentility and wind or cleaning the life out of the music.

Jimmy Lyons, the missionary's son, ex-deejay, ex-dancer, big band nut, had fled San Francisco a couple of years earlier. He opened a general store in Big Sur, down the road from Monterey. He had had it up to here with city noises and city jobs and city driving. The grime of it all, the race of it all.

But jazz does something to the blood. It thickens it, or something; it never leaves. So Jimmy Lyons brought jazz with him to Monterey.

He had to convince the community that jazz (which meant black people and junkies) wouldn't spoil the children, wilt the vegetation, or corrupt the coastline. He had to convince them that jazz would bring in money, culture, decent people.

He aimed at 1957, but by the time he persuaded local merchants and educators and councilmen to let his festival in, it was 1958.

Lyons went to his friends first. He always supported Bay Area jazz musicians. He went after Gerry Mulligan and Paul Desmond and Mort Sahl and Dave Brubeck and Cal Tjader. He went after old friends from his radio days: the Modern Jazz Quartet and Harry James and Dizzy Gillespie. He went after new faces, like the Mastersounds, a group from Seattle featuring the Montgomery Brothers. And he went after old faces, Billie Holiday and Lizzie Miles. He went after Dixieland, Jake Stock's Abalone Stompers, and he went after a symphony conductor, Gregory Millar. And he got them all.

The first year's program reads like this:

Friday, October 3, 1958:
Grounds open at 4 p.m.
Outside stage entertainment Ed Zubov Band, 4–6 p.m.
Main show starts 8:15 p.m. in the Arena.
Special opening and introduction of Master of Ceremonies John Birks "Dizzy" Gillespie.
Jake Stock and the Abalone Stompers featuring the cornet of Pete Dailey.
Burt Bales and the Dixie All Stars with Marty Marsala, trumpet; Skip Morr, trombone; Vince Cattolica, clarinet; Cuz Cousineau, drums; Bill Smith, bass.
Lizzie Miles.
Intermission with piano by Grace Stock.
Louis Armstrong and the All Stars, featuring Velma Middleton.

Saturday Afternoon, October 4:
Grounds open at 11 a.m. with outside entertainment by Claude Gilroy Quintet and Ed Zubov Band.
Jazz Forum at 12:30 p.m. in the Education Building, featuring Louis Armstrong, Dizzy Gillespie, John Lewis, Dave Spears, Albert McCarthy in "Jazz: An International Language." Moderator, Ralph J. Gleason, syndicated jazz columnist and editor "JAZZ, A Quarterly Review."
Main show at 1:30 p.m. in the Arena.
Rudy Salvini and Band share the first half of the program with the Virgil Gonsalves Sextet, Leroy Vinnegar Quartet with Teddy Edwards, Brew Moore and the Dickie Mills Quintet. The second half of the show features the Med Flory Band with such groups as the Mel Lewis-Bill Holman Quintet, Mastersounds, Betty Bennet, Shelly Manne and his Men with Russ Freeman and Herb Geller. The finale will feature the combined Salvini-Flory bands with Pete Rugulo conducting. Pat Henry, KROW disc jockey, will emcee.

Saturday Evening, October 4:
Continuous entertainment on outdoor stage from end of afternoon show until 7 p.m. Exhibits and food and drink concessions open.

Main show begins at 8:30 p.m. in the Arena.

Max Roach Quintet featuring Ray Draper, tuba, and Booker Little, trumpet. Jimmy Giuffre Three with Bobby Brookmeyer and Jim Hall, Gerry Mulligan Quartet with Art Farmer, Ernestine Anderson with Gerry Wiggins, the Modern Jazz Quartet, Cal Tjader Sextet, Dizzy Gillespie Quintet. Plus Sonny Rollins, Buddy De Franco, a Buddy Montgomery, Cal Tjader, Milt Jackson vibes specialty; Dizzy Gillespie with Tjader Afro-Cuban specialty; and a surprise finale. Jimmy Lyons will emcee.

Sunday Afternoon, October 5:

Grounds open at 11 a.m. with continuous entertainment on outside stage.

Exhibit halls and concessions open, with a special Film Forum on jazz scheduled for the Education Building at 12:30.

Afternoon show begins at 1:30 p.m. in the Arena.

The Monterey Jazz Festival Symphony under the direction of Gregory Millar will make its first appearance and Millar will serve as master of ceremonies. The orchestra will play excerpts from Stravinsky, Hindemith and Milhaud.

Dave Brubeck and the Quartet will perform "Summersong" and "G Flat Theme" with the symphony and Howard Brubeck will conduct portions of his "Dialogue for Quartet and Orchestra" and the Quartet will offer "Jazz Impressions of Eurasia." The Modern Jazz Quartet will play the premiere performance of Andre Hodier's "Around the Blues" and Werner Heider's "Divertimento" with the symphony and then perform John Lewis' "Queen's Fancy." Two new selections will also be heard and the finale will be the Pete Phillips "Toccata for Jazz Percussions and Orchestra" featuring Max Roach, Joe Morello and Shelly Manne.

Sunday Evening, October 5:

Evening show starts 8:15 p.m. in the Arena.

Harry James and the new band will be featured during the evening show with comedian Mort Sahl as the Master of Ceremonies. Dave Brubeck and the Quartet, Benny Carter, Billie Holiday appear, and Giuffre-Hall-Brookmeyer premiere their new "Western Suite." The jazz all-stars from Saturday and Sunday evenings will wind up the weekend with a jam session with the James band.

The first Festival was educational as much as it was entertaining. Jazz was still being treated as if it were a silent man behind shades. The official program included an Argot of Jazz, by Elliot Horne (see pg. 154), and biographies of top jazz performers.

* * *

Well, my God, the Festival had everything under the sun. It had comedy and Dixieland and surprises and jam sessions and educational forums and mainstream and far out and special compositions and a symphony and a combination of symphony and jazz and stars and unknowns.

Lyons knew how to put on concerts. He had been doing that nearly all his life, most recently the winter Jazz at Sunset concerts, where Erroll Garner recorded his smash LP,

Program Cover, 1958

"Concert By The Sea." But this was staggering.

Gillespie opened the show. And he popped up, over and over again, with different groups. He closed the Festival with a Latin jam, featuring Cal Tjader and Mongo Santamaria and Willie Bobo.

Dizzy idolized Louis Armstrong. Louis sat in a moving van backstage and held court. Every musician there idolized Louis.

On Saturday afternoon, John Lewis, Diz, Louis and Ralph Gleason defined what jazz was. And on Sunday Mort Sahl introduced Harry James. Sahl had worked a previous concert for Lyons and been scared to go on. He'd paced backstage and thought, "What the hell am I doing here? This crowd doesn't want to hear a monologue. They want to hear jazz." He got on stage and his first bit was 17 minutes. The crowd loved him. Jimmy Lyons was so pleased he bought Sahl two new corduroy jackets at Sears.

Lyons would continue having peculiar, inventive emcees and entre'acts. They became something of a Monterey trademark.

Artistically, that first Festival was untoppable. Probably the most creative line-up of talent and pure jazz information ever put together for a weekend. It made about $600. It was disorganized, frantic and searching. But it did win over the people on the Monterey Peninsula. Monterey and Carmel and Pacific Grove and The Marina and Seaside and "The Gates" and The Valley and Big Sur and the Pacific still stood. The poor remained poor, the rich remained rich. There were no race wars or dope wars. People lived and died that weekend, like they do every weekend. The Festival had put its music in the air, and Jimmy Lyons went home to reorganize for 1959.

Gregory Millar and the Modern Jazz Quartet, 1958

Harry James and his band, 1958

Dave Brubeck, 1958

Lizzy Miles belts out a song, 1958

1959

Lyons proved it. Monterey would support a jazz festival. It already supported the Laguna Seca National Road Races and the Bing Crosby Pro. Am. Golf Tournament and the Pebble Beach Dog Show and the Bach Festival. Lyons paid back his debts and the list of local supporters grew: music stores, liquor stores, motels, radio stations, drive-ins, the newspaper, department stores, drug stores, cleaners, the college. Five thousand people were coming to Monterey to hear jazz. They brought their wallets with them.

When Jimmy Lyons asked John Lewis to be his music director after that first crazy Festival, he assured himself of several things: the respect of musicians; a sort of international flair; a serious, dignified approach to jazz.

Jazz festivals were popping up all over the place in 1958 and 1959. In Boston and Toronto and Chicago. But second annual festivals were as rare then as they are now. No other festival has lasted 20 years in the same place.

The Festival started getting some shape. It wouldn't have that gangbuster approach that the first Festival had but it would have early New Orleans and workshops and a mixture of jazz and classical. And it had something else very special: Lambert, Hendricks and Ross as musical emcees.

The early Monterey audiences were almost all white. Gradually, over the years, the audience has become 60–70% black. Jimmy Lyons, from the beginning, made a conscious effort to integrate his concerts.

The program for 1959:

Friday Evening, October 2 at 8:15 p.m.:
Chris Barber Band: Monty Sunshine, clarinet; Pat Halcox, trumpet; Chris Barber, trombone; Graham Burbidge, drums; Dick Smith, bass; Eddie Smith, banjo; Ottile Patterson, vocals.
(Monty Sunshine did the hit disc of "Petite Fleur.")
Lizzie Miles, with Burt Bales, piano.
George Lewis New Orleans Band: George Lewis, clarinet; Jim Robinson, trombone; Joe Watkins, drums; Alcide Pavageau, bass; Joe Robicheaux, piano; Buddy Bolden Jr., trumpet.
Earl Hines: Earl Hines, piano; Vernon Alley, bass; Mel Lewis, drums.
Jimmy Witherspoon with the Monterey Jazz All Stars: Ben Webster, tenor sax; Coleman Hawkins, tenor sax; Woody Herman, clarinet; Bobby Brookmeyer, trombone; J.J. Johnson, trombone; Earl Hines, piano; Vernon Alley, bass; Mel Lewis, drums.
Lambert, Hendricks & Ross as the musical emcees—Dave Lambert, Jon Hendricks, Annie Ross, with Gildo Mahones, piano; Ike Isaacs, bass; Walter Bolden, drums.

Saturday Afternoon, October 3 at 1:30 p.m.:
Specially Commissioned Jazz Works by John Lewis, J.J. Johnson, Benny Golson, Quincy Jones and Ernie Wilkins.
Woody Herman and the All Stars: Woody Herman, Zoot Sims, Richie Kamuca, Med Florey, Don Lanphere, Bill Perkins, saxes; Conte Candoli, Ray Linn, Bill Chase, Frank Huggins, trumpets; Bobby Brookmeyer, Si Zentner, Bob Smiley, trombones; Mel Lewis, drums; Monte Budwig, bass; Victor Feldman, piano. Charlie Byrd, guitar.
J.J. Johnson and Orchestra.
Coleman Hawkins and Orchestra.
Ben Webster and Orchestra.
Ornette Coleman and Orchestra.
J.J. Johnson, Ornette Coleman and Orchestra.
"Three Saxes": Hawkins, Webster, Coleman and Orchestra.

Saturday Evening, October 3 at 8:15 p.m.:
Woody Herman and the All Stars.
Ernestine Anderson, with the Woody Herman Band.
Modern Jazz Quartet: John Lewis, piano (Festival Musical Consultant); Percy Heath, bass; Connie Kay, drums; Milt Jackson, vibes.
Lambert, Hendricks & Ross (also musical emcees).

Cal Tjader Quintet: Cal Tjader, vibes; Lonnie Hewitt, piano; Willie Bobo, drums; Buddy Catlett, bass; Mongo Santamaria, congo drum; plus Paul Horn, alto sax and flute.

Woody Herman and the All Stars.

Sunday Afternoon, October 4 at 1:30 p.m.:

Six different symphonic brass ensembles to perform new works by John Lewis, Andre Hodier, Werner Heider and J.J. Johnson.

Modern Jazz Quartet.

J.J. Johnson.

Buddy Collette.

Paul Horn.

John Lewis.

Gunther Schuller will conduct "Symphony for Brass and Percussion."

Sunday Evening, October 4 at 7:15 p.m.:

Count Basie and Orchestra with Joe Williams: Snooky Young, Thad Jones, John Anderson, Joe Joe Newman, trumpets; Frank Foster, Frank Wess, Billy Mitchell, Charlie Fowlkes, saxes; Henry Coker, Al Grey, Benny Powell, trombones; rhythm: Freddie Green, guitar; Eddie Jones, bass; Sonny Payne, drums; Count Basie, piano. Vocals by Joe Williams.

Lambert, Hendricks & Ross (also musical emcees).

Oscar Peterson Trio: Oscar Peterson, piano; Ray Brown, bass; Ed Thigpen, drums.

Sarah Vaughan, with the Ronnel Bright Trio.

Count Basie and Orchestra.

* * *

Certain things were already established by the second year. There would be commissioned works each year; there would be freaky, explosive jam sessions (Ornette Coleman, Ben Webster and Coleman Hawkins!), and there would not be thirty acts a night.

It was becoming fashionable at festivals to send musicians out on the bandstand until

Program Cover, 1959

everyone in the crowd was limp with exhaustion. Lewis and Lyons decided that a 35-minute set was adequate for a festival. Each soloist or group would have its best shot, and it would leave six or seven acts to fill a concert.

The biographies included in the 1959 program were limited and selective. There was a long piece on Woody Herman; and Grover Sales' piece on Hendricks, Lambert, and Ross:

"Hendricks writes all the lyrics for the trio and is in a class by himself. . . . Jon has been specially commissioned by the Monterey Jazz Festival to compose lyrics which will serve to introduce the great jazz stars. . . ."

"Lambert calls himself the 'world's oldest living bebop singer.' Originally a swing drummer . . . he is actually the person responsible for the formation of the group. . . ."

"Annie Ross . . . was featured in many of the early Our Gang comedies. Her recording of "Twisted," a child-psychiatric tour de force composed around a tenor sax improvisation by the late Wardell Gray, became an immediate sensation. . . ."

And there was John Hammond's long piece on Count Basie, commemorating Basie's 25th year as a bandleader:

"It was in the fall of 1934 that Bill Basie took over the remnants of the Bennie Moten band.

"Basie's present-day orchestra is a far cry from the nine piece group that rocked the Kansas City Reno Club in the mid-Thirties, and it also has little in common with his first big band, which revolutionized jazz in 1937 with the recording of 'One O'Clock Jump.' Today's Basie band is a polished, virtuoso group of sophisticated, schooled musicians, who concentrate on achieving their effect through intricate arrangements. . . .

"He started on drums, switched to piano, and then took up organ, after listening to Fats Waller at New York's Lincoln Theatre. During the Twenties he worked as [a] pianist . . . in Harlem clubs. . . . In 1928 he joined his first semi-name band, Walter Page's Blue Devils (with vocalist Jimmy Rushing).

"Bennie Moten took over the Blue Devils two years later and installed Basie as second (to Buster Moten) pianist.

". . . It wasn't until Basie took over in 1934 that the orchestra really established an identity of its own. . . . Jo Jones, for instance, had never been with Moten, nor had Lester Young . . . two of the most important cogs in the band first known as Count Basie's. . . .

"It was only after months of experimenting with personnel that the Count Basie orchestra found any measure of public acceptance. 'One O'Clock Jump' was a big factor, but it was the presence of the . . .

soloists (Lester Young, Herschel Evans, Jack Washington, Buck Clayton, Harry Edison, Benny Moten, Dickie Wells, and the historic rhythm section of Basie, Jones, Green and Page) that caused it to be hailed by the general public. Basie's real contribution to jazz was the raising of the sideman to a star. . . .

"A change in management in the late Forties proved disastrous . . . and the early Fifties saw Basie as the leader of a scuffling small combo attempting to compete with the 'bop' groups of the era.

"Today's Basie orchestra stems from 1953, when Willard Alexander resumed his role as manager. . . .

"Along with Duke Ellington, Count Basie is the most durable bandleader in jazz history . . . and I can only hope that the Monterey audience will inspire him to play with the exuberance that has always stimulated his cohorts." (Basie returned to Monterey in 1966, 1968 and 1977.)

The Festival had a unifying theme, an all star big band led by Woody Herman and John Lewis, special compositions and Ornette Coleman. But it lost $12,000. Unlike the first year, no donation would be given to Monterey Peninsula College, and there was serious doubt about the public supporting a festival dedicated to unusual programming. The two afternoon concerts, devoted to music thought of as avant garde, had attracted disappointingly small audiences. The Festival Board of Directors backed Lyons' and Lewis' decision to continue in their direction.

John Lewis told the Board, "The public will come around. It may take five years, but people will start coming to those planned programs of original music during the afternoons."

A Festival that was thought of as experimental and far out would, ten years later, be called stuffy and conservative.

The 1959 program also included a tribute to Billie Holiday, who died soon after her 1958 Festival appearance:

BILLIE

Her enchanted heart, blue, bare
but all of her heart, there,
covered with thin hands
she fronted the meteor-noted band,
stood out with shadow eyes before the
    stand.
She sang slowly the ocean's deeps,
dark girl-queen before her city of fine
    glass;
in her magic throat the dream
    was . . . embalmed,
counterpointed with heavy behind the
    task.
She was a puzzle of beauty,
her face fragmented in its faceted digression,
and there are those
who watched her magic face grow,
moving at phantom and shadow pace
        from this
            to the next
            . . . . session.
                            Kenneth H. Ford

Billie Holiday in her one appearance at Monterey, 1958

Record from 1959 (recorded live at Monterey):
The Spoon Concerts (Jimmy Witherspoon)
Fantasy, 24701.

Left to right: Pony Poindexter, Jon Hendricks, Big Miller on the Monterey stage, 1960

Wes Montgomery, 1960

Sonny Rollins, 1958

Nat and Cannonball Adderley, 1960

1960

1960 was the year of Ellington. Monterey commissioned Ellington to write a piece for the Festival and Ellington came up with "Suite Thursday," based on the works of John Steinbeck. In return, the Festival and program were devoted to Duke Ellington.

Ralph Gleason wrote a program essay about Duke. And the program listed all the extended compositions by Duke Ellington, through 1959.

In addition, the program listed the following people who played and recorded with the Duke Ellington Orchestra, 1925–1960:

Trumpet: William "Cat" Anderson; Louis Bacon; Harold "Shorty" Baker; June Clark; Willie Cook; Fats Ford; Andre Marenghito; John "Dizzy" Gillespie; Shelton Hemphill; Freddie "Posey" Jenkins; Wallace Jones; Taft Jordan; Al Killian; Louis Metcalf; James "Bubber" Miley; Ray Nance (also violin and vocal); Red Rodney; "Jabbo" Smith; Rex Stewart (cornet); Clark Terry; Arthur Whetzel; Charles "Cootie" Williams (also vocal); Francis Williams; Nelson Williams; Gerald Wilson.

Clarinet: Barney Bigard; Jimmy Hamilton; Chauncey Haughton; Rudy Jackson; Prince Robinson.

Soprano Sax: Sidney Bechet.

E Flat Horn: Mercer Ellington.

Trombone: Lawrence Brown; Wilbur de Paris; Matthew Gee, Jr.; Tyree Glenn (also vibes); Jimmy Harrison; Charlie Irvis; Quentin Jackson; Claude Jones; Joe "Tricky Sam" Nanton; John Sanders; Juan Tizol (also valve trombone, arranger); Harry White; Booty Wood; Britt Woodman.

Alto Sax: Benny Carter; Otto "Toby" Harwick; Johnny Hodges (also soprano sax); Hilton Jefferson; Russell Procope (also clarinet); Don Redman; Willie Smith; Rick Henderson.

Tenor Sax: Frank Foster; Joe Garland; Paul Gonsalves; Al Sears; Ben Webster.

Baritone Sax: Harry Carney (also clarinet, bass clarinet); Gerry Mulligan.

Vocalists: Ivy Anderson; Ozzie Bailey; Rosemary Clooney; Baby Cox; Bing Crosby; Kay Davis; Ella Fitzgerald; Sara Ford; Lili Gigi; Jimmy Grissom; Adelaide Hall; Woody Herman; Al Hibbler; Mahalia Jackson; Herb Jeffries; The Mills Brothers; Betty Roche; Jimmy Rushing; Joya Sherill; Ethel Waters; Mae West; Frank Sinatra.

Piano and Composer-Arranger: Duke Ellington; Billy Strayhorn.

Drums: Butch Ballard; Louis Bellson; Dave Black; "Big" Sidney Catlett; Sonny Greer; Joe Jones; Max Roach; Sam Woodyard.

Guitar: Dave Barbour; Teddy Bunn; Fred Guy (also banjo); Lonnie Johnson.

Bass: Aaron Bell; Jimmy Blanton; Jimmy Bryant; Alvin Junior Ragland; Wellman Brand; Jimmy Woode; Bob Haggart; Billy Taylor; Hayes Alvis; Edgar Brown; Joe Shulman; Sid Weiss; Lloyd Trotman; Oscar Pettiford (also cello); Wilson Myers; Wendell Marshall.

* * *

Duke Ellington, like Dizzy Gillespie, would become something of a Monterey regular. People would expect to see certain musicians there every year. Eventually many in the audience would complain that the same faces came back every year. Running a festival has never been a way to win a popularity contest.

This year's two afternoon programs were extraordinary. On Saturday, Monterey continued its serious music presentations with Gunther Schuller's compositions and Ornette Coleman and John Coltrane concerts.

On Sunday afternoon, Jon Hendricks

presented . . . well, what happened was Jimmy Lyons had asked Hendricks to come up with "something about the blues" for Sunday. Hendricks, a talented oral poet and singer and conceiver, came up with Miriam Makeba, Odetta, Jimmy Witherspoon, and the Andrew Sisters Gospel Group, among others, and presented "Evolution of the Blues," a word-music history of blues. Five thousand people sat in the sunny Festival arena and watched Hendricks carry out this wonderful, moving tribute to a music that's been maligned more than any music in America.

The rest of the 1960 program:

Friday Evening, September 23, at 8:15 p.m.:
Andre Previn Trio with Red Mitchell, bass and Frank Capp, drums.

Gerry Mulligan Orchestra, with Nick Travis, Conte Candoli and Don Ferrara, trumpets; Bobby Brookmeyer, Willie Dennis and Allan Raph, trombones; Zoot Sims, Gene Quill, Bobby Donovan, Jim Reider and Gene Allen, saxes; Mel Lewis, drums; Buddy Clarke, bass.

Helen Humes.

J.J. Johnson.

Hendricks, Lambert & Ross, Musical Masters of Ceremonies.

Saturday Afternoon, September 24, at 1:30 p.m.:
"New Music": Gunther Schuller, conductor; John Lewis, commentator. John Coltrane Quartet with Eric Dolphy, Elvin Jones and Wes Montgomery. Ornette Coleman Quartet. Festival String Quartet with Israel Baker, leader; Larry Bunker, vibes; Red Mitchell, bass; Dennis Buddimir, guitar; Frank Capp, drums.

Saturday Evening, September 24, at 8:15 p.m.:
Duke Ellington Orchestra, with Lawrence Brown, "Booty" Wood and Matthew Gee, Jr., trombones; Ray Nance, Andre Marenghito, Willie Cook and Eddie Mullins, trumpets; Russell Procope, Johnny Hodges, Paul Gonsalves, Jimmy Hamilton, Harry Carney, saxes; Sam Woodyard, drums; Aaron Bell, bass.

Lambert, Hendricks & Ross.

Jimmy Rushing.

Julian "Cannonball" Adderley, with Nat Adderley, cornet; Sam Jones, bass; Louis Hayes, drums; Victor Feldman, piano.

Sunday Afternoon, September 25, at 1:30 p.m.:
"Evolution of the Blues Song," conceived and directed by Jon Hendricks, with Lambert, Hendricks & Ross, Odetta, Miriam Makeba, Jimmy Witherspoon, Big Miller and the Children.

Sunday Evening, September 25, at 7:15 p.m.:
Louis Armstrong All-Stars, with Trummy Young, trombone; Billy Kyle, piano; Barney Bigard, clarinet; Danny Barcelona, drums; and Orville Shaw, bass.

Modern Jazz Quartet, with John Lewis, piano; Milt Jackson, vibes; Percy Heath, bass; Connie Kay, drums.

Ornette Coleman Quartet.

Lambert, Hendricks & Ross.

Montgomery Brothers, with Monk Montgomery, bass; Buddy Montgomery, piano; and Wes Montgomery, guitar.

The Festival was set enough in its ways to issue a statement of principles and here's what it included:

1. All programming and selection of performing artists is in the hands of a professional musician (John Lewis), not a booker or promoter.

2. Monterey avoids the hackneyed and the trite by commissioning new works by prominent composers who are exploring the new frontiers of jazz and by organizing special workshop orchestras and units.

3. Monterey introduces important new artists rather than merely "play it safe" with an endless parade of "name" attractions.

4. Nothing will be permitted to interfere with the enjoyment of guests; flashbulbs, rowdyism and similar disturbances that have marred other festivals never have been in evidence in Monterey.

5. The Monterey event is a civic enterprise of the City of Monterey . . . .

6. The Monterey Jazz Festival is a non-profit corporation . . . . All profits are used to establish music scholarships at Monterey Peninsula College.

7. Monterey encourages the study and practice of jazz in colleges and high schools. Each year the Festival sponsors a statewide competition of high school big bands and small units at Monterey Peninsula College.

8. Monterey presents a true *festival*, not merely an unrelated series of concerts.

The seventh one, the encouraging of high school and college kids to play jazz, that's the one Jimmy Lyons really would stick to. That's the one that won his heart, the one that Monterey would eventually become: a Festival that produced staggeringly good youngsters playing their cans off.

Louis Armstrong with Barney Bigard, 1960

Lambert, Hendricks and Ross, musical emcees, 1960

Duke Ellington, left, and his Orchestra, with Paul Gonsalves on sax and tap dancer Bunny Briggs, 1960

A song from Helen Humes, 1960

1961

Last year belonged to Ellington and this year belonged to Dizzy Gillespie. Two compositions were written for Dizzy for the Festival: Boris "Lalo" Schifrin's "Gillespiana Suite" and J.J. Johnson's "Perceptions." (Lalo Schifrin was Dizzy's piano player.)

It was a great tribute to a man who has been one of the driving forces of modern jazz. Because Dizzy is so comic and relaxed and unpretentious and because he swings so easily, people tend to forget what a wonderful, serious musician he is.

The program started off, 8:15 p.m. on a Friday night, with Duke Ellington as the Master of Ceremonies. (He would also act as the intermission piano player. It was becoming apparent that musicians were getting a kick playing at Monterey.)

Duke introduced the following acts:

Terry Gibbs Big Band, with Bob Edmundson, Harry Betts, Frank Rosolino and Ken Schroyer, trombones; Al Porcino, Conte Candoli, Ray Triscari, Ray Linn, trumpets; Joe Maine, Charlie Kennedy, Bill Perkins, Richie Kamuca, Jack Nimitz, saxes; Buddy Clark, bass; Mel Lewis, drums; Lou Levy, piano.

John Coltrane Quartet, with McCoy Tyner, piano; Elvin Jones, drums; Reggie Workman, bass.

Modern Mainstream Set, with Johnny Hodges, Dizzy Gillespie, Ben Webster, Harry Carney, Lawrence Brown, Stuff Smith, Ray Nance, Ralph Sutton and the Rhythm Section.

The Blues Song, with Jimmy Rushing and Big Miller.

(The evening had its share of jams. Evenings at Monterey would be filled, more and more, with jams; star musicians getting together for 45 minutes and playing a ballad, a blues and an uptempo thing.)

On Saturday afternoon, 1:30, the Festival gave the day to Duke Ellington. The Ellington Orchestra, with Ray Nance, Willie Cook, Cat Anderson, Eddie Mullins, trumpets; Lawrence Brown, Bo Connors, Lou Blackburn, trombones;

Johnny Hodges, Russell Procope, Paul Gonsalves, Jimmy Hamilton, Harry Carney, saxes; Aaron Bell, bass; Sam Woodyard, drums.

Saturday Evening, Duke Ellington again was the Master of Ceremonies:

J.J. Johnson with Brass Choir.

Carmen McRae and her Trio.

Dizzy Gillespie Quintet, with Lew Wright on alto and flute; Lalo Schifrin, piano; Chuck Lampkin, drums; Bob Cunningham, bass.

Joe Carroll and Dizzy Gillespie.

George Shearing Quintet, with Armando Perazza, Latin drums.

George Shearing with J.J. Johnson, and the Festival Brass Choir.

Sunday afternoon, September 24, at 1:30 p.m. (Dizzy's day):

The Festival Brass Orchestra under the direction of Gunther Schuller and starring Dizzy Gillespie.

The West Coast Premiere of Lalo Schifrin's "Gillespiana." (A Tunisian fantasy based on Dizzy Gillespie's "Night in Tunisia.")

The World Premiere of "Perceptions" by J.J. Johnson.

(Johnson said of the piece, "Dizzy had in mind a concert type piece. . . . His talent and abilities as a musician are so complete, so gigantic, and so colossal, that it would be nearly impossible to write a piece that really and truly gave evidence of the wide range of his capabilities.")

Sunday Evening, September 24, at 7:15 p.m.:

Duke Ellington, Master of Ceremonies.

Odetta sings the songs of Bessie Smith and Ma Rainey.

Dave Brubeck Quartet, featuring Paul Desmond, alto sax, with Joe Morello, drums, and Eugene Wright, bass.

Duke Ellington and Orchestra.

* * *

Saxmen, left to right: Paul Gonsalves, Johnny Hodges, Russell Procope, Harry Carney, 1968

The Brass Ensemble, led by Gunther Schuller, consisted of seven trumpets, four trombones, four French horns, two tubas, two harps and percussion.

Schuller, 35 at the time (he's now dean of the New England Conservatory of Music), was a leader of what was called "Third Stream," a mixture of jazz and classical music. He was good friends with John Lewis and had been performing and writing for Monterey since 1959.

He was giving a touch of class to the Festival. The American Salzberg, it was being called.

Monterey was also starting to make some money. In '61 the Festival netted $12,500. Of that, $2,000 went to Monterey Peninsula College, $5,800 went to old debts, and $4,700 went to finance the 1962 Festival.

Acts were cheaper than they are now. But it was still costly to put on a Festival. The John Coltrane Quartet cost $950; the Terry Gibbs Big Band, $2,500; Carmen McRae, $1,500; George Shearing Quintet, $2,000. It cost nearly $3,000 to put on "Gillespiana."

A Festival today with equal star appeal would cost more than double.

John Coltrane, 1960

Odetta in "Evolution of the Blues Song," 1960

Johnny Hodges and Ben Webster, 1961

1962

Saxophonist Benny Carter took over the job of musical director because John Lewis was on a long South American tour. So Carter made Saturday afternoon a salute to the sax, with Paul Desmond, Stan Getz, Ben Webster and Gerry Mulligan among others wandering around the stage, in what amounted to a giant saxophone jam session.

But there were problems amidst the frolic.

The Festival was getting too successful for the 5,000 seat arena in the fairgrounds. So the State of California appropriated funds to replace the wooden stands of the Horse Shoe Arena with a modern 7,100 seat arrangement. It was supposed to be finished by the third week in September, the official date for the Festival. But a long strike in the building trade union interrupted the banging. A temporary arena was set up 300 yards away, on the fairgrounds.

Then the horror happened; what everybody had been expecting to happen happened. Chaos. Rowdy rotten chaos. Non-paying customers milled around the arena, on the fairgrounds, and got restless. People brought their bongos and congos and started competing with the concerts, and getting drunk and wanting trouble.

It never reached a really ugly head, like the Newport riots of 1969, but it did cause the Festival Board to close off the fairgrounds to "non-listeners" for future concerts. Next year you'd need a ticket to set foot on the lush, green, soft-winded fairgrounds. There's a lot of grounds here, with old wood buildings and a faint manure drift that never leaves. And now it would be reserved, on the third weekend, for the Monterey jazz audience—an audience that was becoming larger, certainly, but also more specialized, more in love with the kind of music Jimmy Lyons loved, big band music and hard swing. It would have little patience for experimental music.

The program began Friday Evening, September 21, 8:15 p.m. with "The Swingers":

Earl "Fatha" Hines, piano; Ben Webster, tenor sax; Benny Carter, alto sax; Rex Stewart, cornet; Bill Harris, trombone; Stuff Smith, violin; Conte Candoli, trumpet; Mel Lewis, drums; Buddy Clark, bass. (Organized and conducted by Benny Carter.)

And followed with:

"The Blues Song," with Helen Humes, Jimmy Rushing, Jimmy Witherspoon, accompanied by "The Swingers."

Earl "Fatha" Hines, entr'acte solo pianist.

The Stan Getz Quartet, with Jimmy Raney, guitar; Tommy Williams, bass; Al Harewood, drums.

Earl "Fatha" Hines entr'acte solo pianist.

"The New Continent," a World Premiere of a work by Boris "Lalo" Schifrin, commissioned by the Monterey Jazz Festival. A Divertimento for Jazz Trumpet and Orchestra in Six Movements with Dizzy Gillespie, solo trumpet; Lalo Schifrin, pianist-composer; Benny Carter, conductor of the Workshop Orchestra; Al Porcino, Conte Candoli, Stu Williamson, Ray Triscari, trumpets; Henry Schroyer, Bob Edmundson, Mike Barone, Dick Noel, trombones; James Moody, Phil Woods, alto saxophones; Bill Perkins, Charlie Kennedy, tenor saxophones; Bill Hood, baritone saxophone; Thomas Chestnut, Kensey Stewart, French horns; Red Callender, tuba; Buddy Clark, Christopher White, string bass; Larry Bunker, vibraharp; Al Hendrickson, guitar; Emil Richards, tympani; Francisco Aquabella, Rudy Collins, Latin percussion; Mel Lewis, drums.

Saturday Afternoon, September 22, at 1:30 p.m.:
"Salute to the Sax"

A program commissioned by the MJF in honor of the Belgian inventor of the saxophone, Adolph Sax. Organized and composed by the Festival's Acting Musical Director, Benny Carter. Among the participating saxophonists will be: Benny Carter, Paul Desmond, James Moody, Phil Woods, alto saxophones; Stan Getz, Charlie Kennedy, Bill Perkins, Ben Webster, tenor saxophones; Bill Hood, Gerry Mulligan, baritone and bass saxophones.

Saturday Evening, September 22, at 8:15 p.m.:

Quincy Jones and the Monterey Jazz Festival Orchestra in a program of new arrangements by Quincy Jones, with Quincy Jones, Al Porcino, Stu Williamson, Conte Candoli, Ray Triscari, trumpets; Henry Schroyer, Bob Edmundson, Mike Barone, Dick Noel, trombones; James Moody, Phil Woods, Bill Perkins, Charlie Kennedy, Bill Hood, reeds; Christopher White, bass; Rudy Collins, drums; Al Hendrickson, guitar.

Vince Guaraldi Trio, entr'acte piano, with Vince Guaraldi, piano; Eddie Coleman, bass; Collin Bailey, drums.

Gerry Mulligan Quartet, with Bobby Brookmeyer, valve trombone and piano; Gus Johnson, drums; Bill Crow, bass.

Vince Guaraldi Trio, entr'acte piano.

Lambert, Hendricks and Bavan Trio, with Dave Lambert, Jon Hendricks and Yolande Bavan (who replaced Annie Ross).

Ted Curson, his West Coast debut. (He was selected by the Festival as a "new star" of 1962. He didn't go over. Nobody knew who he was. He would come back 15 years later and steal the show.)

Dave Brubeck Quartet, with Paul Desmond, alto sax; Eugene Wright, bass; Joe Morello, drums.

Vince Guaraldi Trio, entr'acte piano.

Quincy Jones and the MJF Orchestra.

Sunday Afternoon, September 23, at 1:30 p.m.:

"The Relatives of Jazz," organized and presented by Dizzy Gillespie to show the influence of diverse cultures on American music, with the Dizzy Gillespie Quintet (Gillespie, trumpet, narrative, vocal and choreography; James Moody, alto, tenor, baritone saxophone, and flute; Lalo Schifrin, piano; Christopher White, bass; Rudy Collins, drums. And these relatives: Yaffa Yarkoni, Israeli folk singer; Bola Sete, Brazilian guitarist; Francisco Aquabella, Latin percussion; and the Virgin Island Steel Band.)

Sunday Evening, September 23, at 7:15 p.m. sharp:

Dizzy Gillespie and the Monterey Brass Ensemble.

Jeanne Lee and Ran Blake, entr'acte.

"The Real Ambassadors" (excerpts), an original musical production, with music and lyrics by Dave and Iola Brubeck, featuring Louis Armstrong, Carmen McRae, Dave Brubeck, Lambert, Hendricks and Yolande, with Billy Kyle, Trummy Young, Joe Darensbourg, Billy Cronk, Danny Barcelona, Joe Morello, Eugene Wright.

Jeanne Lee and Ran Blake, entr'acte.

Louis Armstrong and his All-Stars, with Jewel Brown, vocal; Trummy Young, trombone and vocal; Joe Darensbourg, clarinet; Billy Kyle, piano; Bill Cronk, bass; Danny Barcelona, drums.

* * *

Benny Carter had put together a fine, swinging Festival. He had been at the first Festival, playing behind Billie Holiday, and he had brought together Louis Armstrong and Dizzy Gillespie (Dizzy still adored Louis; Louis thought Dizzy was one of those young Turks, but he respected him); he had made Earl Hines an entr'acte pianist and had Mulligan and Brubeck in the same evening.

The themes of the Festival—the influences on American jazz and in turn its influence on the world—would be something Monterey would continue developing: the meeting place and cauldron for international jazz.

Between shows—Dizzy Gillespie and Jimmy Rushing, 1963

Gerry Mulligan, 1960

1963

These were the swollen years at Monterey. Swollen in talent, and swollen in prestige. Monterey was making West Coast jazz reputable.

Two of the giants of modern jazz made their Monterey debuts this year: Thelonious Monk and Miles Davis, two of the most mysterious brilliant men playing music. Monk, the silent, gentle man in a long overcoat arrived with his wife, Nellie. Nellie does all the talking for Monk. And Miles arrived with his gravelly voice, a Ferrari and his strange temper intact.

Miles started the program on a Friday evening at 9 p.m. with Herbie Hancock, piano; George Coleman, tenor sax; Arthur Tony Williams, drums; Ron Carter, bass.

The rest of the program:

The Modern Jazz Quartet: John Lewis, piano; Milton Jackson, vibraharp; Percy Heath, bass; Connie Kay, drums.

Jack Teagarden and Pee Wee Russell with Gerry Mulligan, Joe Sullivan, Charlie Teagarden, guests, and the American premiere of the Japanese tenor sax and flute star, "Sleepy" Matsumoto. (It was said of Matsumoto that he had the only white Thunderbird in Japan. It was the beginning of a long relationship between Jimmy Lyons and Japan; when American interest in the Festival would wane, Japanese jazz lovers would be just starting to get excited about Jimmy Lyons' Festival.)

Lambert, Hendricks and Bavan, with the Gildo Mahones trio.

Gerald Wilson and the All-Star Festival Orchestra, with Carmell Jones, Harold Land, Teddy Edwards and Joe Pass.

Saturday Afternoon, September 21, at 1:30 p.m.:
The Drums of Ghana, with Robert Ayitee and Robert Bonsu.

The Elmer Snowden Trio, with Elmer Snowden, banjo; Darnell Howard, clarinet; and George "Pops" Foster, bass. (Miles' drummer, Tony Williams, 17, sat in with these old New Orleans swing musicians, and had the time of his life.)

Turk Murphy and the Earthquake McGoon Jazz Band.

The Andrews Sisters and the Gospel Song.

Joe Sullivan, solo pianist.

Jack Teagarden, Pee Wee Russell, Gerry Mulligan, Charlie Teagarden, Joe Sullivan and the Festival Swing Band.

Gerald Wilson and the All-Star Festival Orchestra: Gerald Wilson, Johnny Audino, Jules Chakin, Carmell Jones, Freddy Hill, trumpets; Bob Edmonson, John Ewing, Lester Robertson, Kenny Schroyer, trombones; Joe Maine, Jimmy Woods, Harold Land, Teddy Edwards, Jack Nimitz, saxes; Jack Wilson, piano; Joe Pass, guitar; Jimmy Bond, bass; Nick Ceroli, drums.

Saturday Evening, September 21, at 8:15 p.m.:
The Gerry Mulligan Quartet with Bobby Brookmeyer, valve trombone and piano; Bill Crow, bass; Gus Johnson, drums.

The Thelonious Monk Quartet, with Charlie Rouse, tenor sax.

Helen Merrill, vocalist.

Jon Hendricks.

Gerald Wilson and the All-Star Festival Orchestra.

Sunday Afternoon, September 22, at 1:30 p.m.:
John Lewis (back as Musical Consultant this year), presents a special program of "New Music."

Thelonious Monk with Festival Guests.

Laurindo Almeida, guitar, joins the Modern Jazz Quartet.

Gerry Mulligan and guests.

Laurindo Almeida, solo guitar.

Gerald Wilson and the All-Star Festival Orchestra.

The Drums of Ghana, with Robert Ayitee and Robert Bonsu.

Sunday Evening, September 22, at 7:15 p.m. sharp.
Carmen McRae, Mistress of Ceremonies.

Harry James and his Orchestra.

Dizzy Gillespie Quintet, featuring James Moody.

The Dave Brubeck Quartet, with Paul Desmond, alto sax, and Joe Morello, drums. Jimmy Witherspoon.

* * *

In some ways this Festival was as crazy and creative as the first. It had a freaky mixture of soloists, big bands, modern music and Dixieland. On Saturday there was a symposium titled "What Happened to Dixieland?" with the Teagardens, Pee Wee Russell and Don De Michael, editor of *Down Beat* magazine.

It had many new faces and many familiar ones. John Lewis was back. There was new music and the MJQ and there was out and out insanity and dancing on the stage (Monk) and three great trumpet players—Miles, Dizzy and Harry James.

There was a moving afternoon moment when the whole Teagarden family was reunited on stage and played the audience to tears. Jack Teagarden would be dead by the next Festival.

Lyons was taking a chance bringing so much old jazz to the Festival and it paid off. The year before he brought "Fatha" Hines before the crowd and the crowd loved the incredibly facile Hines. This year it was the Teagardens and Turk Murphy.

The program supplied biographies of all the musicians making Monterey debuts. Among them:

Laurindo Almeida, a Brazilian guitarist who played Bossa Nova and the classics. Jack Teagarden, one of the most influential trombone players in jazz. He played in fast legato lines and influenced Tommy Dorsey and Glenn Miller and J.C. Higginbotham, among others.

Joe Sullivan, who used to play intermissions at a place called the Club Hangover in San Francisco. He came out of Chicago in the 1920s and played behind Bing Crosby in the '30s.

The Arena had been expanded to seat 7,000, and it was packed. Monterey was becoming the place to be on that third weekend of September. Musicians would plan West Coast gigs around the Festival.

Jazz was spreading across the country and Monterey was helping spread it. This was before the troubled late 60s, when jazz would start splitting up into the screechers versus the swingers, expressive theatre versus the old impressionism, the new cats versus the old cats. Monterey would never buy the avant garde. Lyons thought his audiences wouldn't stand for it. His Jazz Festival would become a specialized jazz festival, and his tickets would sell faster and faster.

Pee Wee Russell, 1963

Carmen McRae, 1963

Harry James, 1963

1964

The chief eccentric of modern jazz showed up at this Festival: Charlie Mingus. He brought a fine sextet, played his heart out, recorded his set, and everything was fine. He would come back the following year disgruntled and distrustful, play an abbreviated set, and march off the stage miserable.

The seventh year also kicked off blues shows on Saturday afternoons. From here on out the Festival would try to feature blues on Saturday afternoons; it would become the loosest part of the Festival. Saturday afternoons would begin selling out faster than any other show.

This was also the year that post-show jam sessions became popular. For three bucks you could get a ticket into the exhibit hall late Friday and Saturday nights and hear more music, unscheduled, unrehearsed. People took a long time getting glutted. The city of Monterey closed up early. So jam sessions watered the tongues. Over the years, people would lose their taste for post-jams and they would just go home to bed.

The program started on a Friday evening, September 18, 9 p.m., with Miles Davis and his Quintet, with Wayne Shorter, tenor sax; Herbie Hancock, piano; Ron Carter, bass; Tony Williams, drums.
And continued with:
Pee Wee Russell and his All-Stars, with Pee Wee Russell, clarinet; Buck Clayton, trumpet; Vic Dickenson, trombone; Bud Freeman, tenor sax; Dick Cary, piano; Red Callender, bass; Earl Palmer, drums.
Art Farmer and his Quartet, with Art Farmer, trumpet and fluegelhorn; Steve Kuhn, piano; Pete La Rocca, drums; Steve Swallow, bass.
Gerry Mulligan, "musician-at-large," with Gerry Mulligan, baritone sax, piano, emcee and prime mover.

Jon Hendricks and Company, with Jon Hendricks, Don Chastain, Pat Harris, accompanied by the Gildo Mahones Trio, with Gildo Mahones, piano; George Tucker, bass; Sonny Brown, drums.

Saturday afternoon, September 19 at 1:30 p.m.:
"The Blues—Right Now!" as conceived by Jon Hendricks.
Joe Williams.
Big Joe Turner.
Lou Rawls.
Roy Gaines.
"Big Mama" Willie Mae Thornton.
Washboard Willie.
Homesick James.
Hank Crawford and His Orchestra.

Saturday Evening, September 19, at 8:15 p.m.:
Duke Ellington and his Famous Orchestra, featuring William "Cat" Anderson, Cootie Williams, Nathan Woodard, Herbert Jones, trumpets; Buster Cooper, Lawrence Brown, Charles Connors, trombones; Russell Procope, Johnny Hodges, Harry Carney, James Hamilton, Paul Gonsalves, saxophones; John Lamb, bass; Sam Woodyard, drums; Duke Ellington, piano.
Horace Silver and his Quintet, with Horace Silver, pianist, composer; Carmell Jones, trumpet; Rod Humphries, drums; Theodore Snow, bass; Joe Hudson, tenor sax.
The Modern Jazz Quartet, with John Lewis, piano; Milt Jackson, vibraharp; Percy Heath, bass; Connie Kay, drums.
Gerry Mulligan, "musician-at-large."
Jon Hendricks and Company, with Jon Hendricks, Don Chastain, Pat Harris, accompanied by the Gildo Mahones Trio.
Carol Sloane, vocalist.

Sunday Afternoon, September 20, at 1:30 p.m.:
World Premieres of new compositions by Charles Mingus and Thelonious Monk, with the Festival Ensemble under the direction of Buddy Collette.

Charles Mingus and his Sextet, with Charles Mingus, bass, composer; Booker Ervin, tenor sax; Jackie Byard, piano; Lonnie Hillyer, trumpet; Charles McPherson, alto sax; Dannie Richmond, drums.

Thelonious Monk and his Quartet, with Thelonious Monk, piano, composer; Charlie Rouse, tenor sax; Butch Warren, bass; Ben Riley, drums.

The Festival Workshop Ensemble, Buddy Collette, director, saxes and flute; with Lou Blackburn, trombone; Jack Nimitz, baritone sax; Bobbie Bryan, trumpet; Melvin Moore, trumpet.

Sunday Evening, September 20, at 7:15 p.m. sharp:

Woody Herman and the 1964 Herman Herd, with Andy McGhee, Raoul Romera, Gary Klein and Tom Anastos, reeds; Bill Chase, Bill Hunt, Gerry Lamy, Larry Ford and Dusko Gojkovic, trumpets; Phil Wilson, Henry Southall and Bob Stroup, trombones; Jake Hanna, drums; Chuck Andrus, bass; Nat Pierce, piano; and featuring Joe Carroll, chanteur.

Dizzy Gillespie and his Quintet, with Dizzy Gillespie, trumpet, composer, vocal, dancer, Latin percussion, emcee; James Moody, alto and tenor sax, flute; Christopher White, bass; Rudy Collins, drums; Kenneth Barron, piano.

Vince Guaraldi-Bola Sete Quartet, with Vince Guaraldi, piano; Bola Sete, guitar; Benny Barth, drums; Tom Beeson, bass.

Jon Hendricks and Company, accompanied by the Gildo Mahones Trio.

* * *

In one weekend there was Miles, Dizzy, Monk, Mingus, Bags (Milt Jackson), Mulligan, Woody Herman, Duke. It was an incredible Festival. There, again, were new compositions by Monk and Mingus, featured, oddly, in the afternoon. Anything that smelled of new music was stuck in the afternoon. Evenings were reserved for good time, less intense music.

Bringing the blues to a jazz festival was a wonderful tribute to the men who are the folk artists of jazz, the blues musicians. Jazz is like classical music: it's technical and difficult to play and requires a listening sophistication. But blues is the working man's music; it's raw and gutsy and spoken.

It wasn't evident yet, but Monterey was getting into a rut. The same faces, no matter how beautiful the faces, were reappearing: Dizzy and Mulligan and Duke and Jon Hendricks and the MJQ. It was becoming something of a cliquey festival. A lot of musicians weren't getting invited or weren't interested. It was too mainstream.

There were some new faces. Horace Silver was making his debut. (Silver had worked with Stan Getz and Coleman Hawkins and Lester Young and Oscar Pettiford and Art Blakey.) And all the blues musicians were making their first appearances. Carol Sloane, a singer, was here for the first time, and Lou Rawls, 25, was never here before. Still, there wasn't that new blood excitement. The surprises weren't stunning.

The only recording made this year was "Mingus at Monterey" (Charles Mingus), on Mingus Records (JWS-00 002). It sold a lot of records. It also became the object of a beef between Mingus and Lyons. Mingus was going to sell the records at Monterey the following year, in one of the arts and crafts booths along the fairgrounds walk. The records arrived late and Mingus blamed the man in charge. He cut his set to one song.

Big Mama Willie Mae Thornton, 1964

Thelonious Monk, 1964

Bola Sete, 1964

Charlie Mingus, 1964

Cootie Williams, 1964

1965

The Festival had established itself as a solid mainstream festival. This year, as in other years, the excitement would come from the afternoon shows.

The theme for the Festival was "The Tribute to the Trumpet." Themes became sort of handles for Festivals. More often than not they worked against the creative charge; they tended to tie things in too neat a package.

The program, Friday evening, September 17, 9 p.m. began with the host Dizzy Gillespie. And continued:

Gil Fuller and the Monterey Jazz Festival Orchestra, Gil Fuller, leader and arranger; Ray Copeland, Clark Terry, Harry "Sweets" Edison, Freddy Hill, Melvin Moore, trumpets; Lester Robinson, Francis "Bob" Fitzpatrick, Dick Hyde (tuba), trombones; Allan Robinson, Gale Robinson, Herman LeBow, Sam Cassano, French horns; Gabriel Baltazar, Buddy Collette (flute, clarinet), William E. Green, Carrington Visor, Jr. (flute), Jack Nimitz, saxes; Phil Moore III, piano; Earl Palmer, drums; Bob West, bass; Bobby Hutcherson, vibes.

Rex Stewart, cornet, "Echoes of Ellington."

Mary Stallings, vocalist.

Dizzy Gillespie Quintet, with Dizzy Gillespie, trumpet; James Moody, alto and tenor sax and flute; Kenny Barron, piano; Chris White, bass; Rudy Collins, drums. With the Monterey Jazz Festival Orchestra.

Louis Armstrong and his All-Stars, with Louis Armstrong, trumpet; Billy Kyle, piano; Tyree Glenn, trombone and vibes; Buster Bailey, clarinet; Danny Barcelona, drums; George Catlett, bass.

Saturday Afternoon, September 18, at 1:30 p.m.:

Rebel Voices — A Presentation of New Music.

Gil Fuller and the Monterey Jazz Festival Orchestra, in a performance of "Abstract Realities," a composition by Russ Garcia.

The Denny Zeitlin Trio, with Dr. Denny Zeitlin, piano; Charlie Haden, bass; Jerry Granelli, drums.

The John Handy Quintet, with John Handy III, alto sax; Terry Clarke, drums; Donald Thompson, bass; Michael White, violin; Jerry Hahn, guitar.

The Charles Mingus Octet — "New Music for Monterey" — with Charles Mingus, bass; Garnet Brown, trombone; Howard Johnson, tuba; Jimmy Owen, trumpet; Lonnie Hillyer, trumpet; Hobart Dotson, trumpet; Charles McPherson, alto sax; Dannie Richmond, drums.

The Mingus portion might have been a disaster, but the John Handy set was electrifying. The quintet's version of "Spanish Lady" was jolting. And the band was offered, and accepted, a record contract from John Hammond and Columbia as soon as they walked off the stage. This set was recorded and released as "John Handy Recorded Live at the Monterey Jazz Festival" (Columbia, CA-9262).

Saturday Evening, September 18, at 8:15 p.m.:

Gil Fuller and the Monterey Jazz Festival Orchestra, featuring Dizzy Gillespie, trumpet: Reminiscences with Dizzy.

Anita O'Day, vocalist, with the Phil Moore Quintet, featuring Clark Terry, trumpet; Phil Moore III, piano; Earl Palmer, drums; Bob West, bass; Bobby Hutcherson, vibes.

Earl "Fatha" Hines, pianist.

Duke Ellington and his Famous Orchestra, with Special Guest Stars; Edward Kennedy Ellington, leader, piano; Louis Bellson, drums; Cootie Williams, Cat Anderson, Mercer Ellington, Herbie Jones, trumpets; Lawrence Brown, Charles Connors, Buster Cooper, trombones; Johnny Hodges, Russell Procope (clarinet), Paul Gonsalves, Jimmy Hamilton (clarinet), Harry Carney (clarinet), saxes; John Lamb, bass.

Sunday Afternoon, September 19, at 1:30 p.m.:

"Trumpets" with Dizzy Gillespie, Clark Terry, Henry "Red" Allen.

Mary Lou Williams, pianist and composer, with the Monterey Jazz Festival Orchestra and the Monterey Jazz Festival Singers: Tom Kenny, Sally Stevens, Vangie Carmichael, Sue Allen, Diana Lee, Chuck Kelly, Joe Pryor, Bill Brown, in a special Sunday performance, "Jazz Music in the Liturgy," and other selections.

World Premiere — music written and arranged by Gil Fuller — Gil Fuller and the Monterey Jazz Festival Orchestra, featuring Dizzy Gillespie, "On the Road to Monterey" and "Angel City Suite."

Sunday Evening, September 19 at 7:15 p.m. (early curtain):

Harry James and his new Swingin' Band, featuring Buddy Rich on drums, Harry James, leader and trumpet; Nick Buono, Fred Koyen, Anton Scodwell, Thomas Porello, trumpets; Joseph Cadena, Ray Simms, David Wheeler, trombones; Corky Corcoran, James Carter (flute), Joe Riggs, Richard Kastel, Robert Achilles (clarinet), saxes; Jack Perciful, piano; Tom Kelly, bass; Ernie Andrews, vocalist.

The Dizzy Gillespie Quintet.

Ethel Ennis, vocalist.

Cal Tjader Quintet, with Cal Tjader, vibes; Johnny Rae, drums; Terry Hilliard, bass; Al Zulaica, piano; Armando Perazza, conga.

Harry James and his new Swingin' Band.

Dizzy Gillespie was the musical consultant this year. It was also the year Dizzy told his audience that he would not run for President after all; he just didn't have the time.

In spite of all the people being overlooked for the Festival—Pharoah Sanders, Cecil Taylor, Roland Kirk, the Art Ensemble, for example—a lot were being invited—Anita O'Day, who in earlier years sang with Kenton and Gene Krupa; and Denny Zeitlin, a practicing psychiatrist in San Francisco; Mary Lou Williams, who could play serious music and swing like mad; and the returnees: "Fatha" Hines, Ellington, Dizzy, Harry James, Louis Armstrong. The Monterey audience was now expecting to see certain people each year. They would have seen Miles Davis again this year, but he broke his leg and had to cancel.

John Handy

Rex Stewart, 1965

Anita O'Day, 1965

Buddy Rich on drums, 1965

Michael White, John Handy, 1965

Jon Hendricks and Dizzy Gillespie rehearse a number, 1965

1966

This was the year Lyons extended, dipping into the new San Francisco pop scene and coming up with the Jefferson Airplane and the Paul Butterfield Blues Band. Lyons knew of the Airplane because he had hired them in the summer to work a society pool party. The blues-pop show on Saturday included Muddy Waters, Jimmy Rushing and Memphis Slim.

Elvin Jones came with his quartet and scared everybody to death with his Doberman. Dobermans were scarier then.

It was also the Festival of two exceptional pianists, completely different. Keith Jarrett, 17 years old, came on with Charles Lloyd and played inside the piano with his nose, fingers, elbows. People backstage were grabbing each other and slapping hands. And Joe Zawinul introduced his incredibly soulful "Mercy Mercy" with the Cannonball Adderley Quintet.

Ray Brown was taking John Lewis' place as musical director.

Friday Evening, September 16, at 9 p.m.:
Gil Evans and the Monterey Jazz Festival All-Star Orchestra: leader and arranger, pianist, Gil Evans; Hobart Dotson, Johnny Coles, trumpets; Howard Johnson, tuba; Billy Harper, Willie Green, Jay Migliori, saxes; Ken Schroyer, bass trombone; Richard Perissi, Enrico Sigismonti, French horns; Ray Brown, bass and cello; Don Moore, bass; Elvin Jones, drums.

The Dave Brubeck Quartet, with Dave Brubeck, piano; Paul Desmond, alto saxophone; Gene Wright, bass; Joe Morello, drums.

The Count Basie Orchestra, with Count Basie, piano; Bill Henderson, vocalist; Eddie "Lockjaw" Davis, Eric Dixon, Bobby Plater, Charles Fowlkes, Marshall Royal, saxophones; Grover Mitchell, Bill Hughes, Richard Boone, trombones; Sonny Cohn, Albert Aarons, Gene Goe, Roy Eldridge, trumpets; Freddie Green, guitar; Norman Keenan, bass; Rufus Jones, drums.

Gerry Mulligan, baritone saxophone, artist-at-large.

Saturday Afternoon, September 17, at 1:30 p.m.:
"Blues All the Way," Jon Hendricks, host and narrator.

The Jon Hendricks Trio, with Jon Hendricks, vocalist; Larry Vuckovich, piano; Bob Maize, bass; Clarence Becton, drums.

Big Mama Willie Mae Thornton, accompanied by Piney Clark, guitar; James Brown, piano.

Shakey Horton, accompanied by the Jon Hendricks Trio.

Memphis Slim.

Muddy Waters and his Band: Muddy Waters, guitar, vocals; Sammy Longhorn, Georgie Boy, guitars; Otis Spann, piano; George Smith, mouth organ; Mack Arnold, Fender bass; James Day, drums.

Jimmy Rushing.

The Paul Butterfield Blues Band, with Paul Butterfield, harmonica; Mike Bloomfield, Elvin Bishop, guitars; Mark Naftalin, organ; Jerome Arnold, electric bass; Billy Davenport, drums.

Jefferson Airplane, with Marty Balin, Signe Anderson, lead vocalists; Jorma Kaukonen and Paul Kantner, guitars, Jack Casady, bass; Spencer Dryden, drums.

Saturday Evening, September 17, at 8:15 p.m.:
Gil Evans and the Monterey Jazz Festival All-Star Orchestra. Featuring guest soloists: Julian "Cannonball" Adderley, alto saxophone; Gerry Mulligan, baritone saxophone; Bola Sete, guitar; Ray Brown, bass and cello; Elvin Jones, drums; Booker Ervin, tenor saxophone.

The Cannonball Adderley Quintet, with Julian "Cannonball" Adderley, alto saxophone; Nat Adderley, cornet; Joe Zawinul, piano; Victor Gaskin, bass; Roy McCurdy, drums.

The Elvin Jones-Joe Henderson Quartet, with Elvin Jones, drums, Joe Henderson, tenor saxophone; Bobby Hutcherson, vibes; Don Moore, bass.

The Bola Sete Trio, with Bola Sete, guitar; Sebastian Neto, bass; Palinho, drums.

Carol Sloane, vocalist.

Left to right: Cannonball and Nat Adderley, Joe Zawinul, 1969

Sunday Afternoon, September 18, at 1:30 p.m.:

The Don Ellis 21-piece Workshop Orchestra, with Don Ellis, Glenn Stuart, Alan Weight, Ed Warren, Paul Lopez, trumpets; Dave Wells, Ron Meyers, Terry Woodson, trombones; Ruben Leon, Tom Scott, Ira Schulman, Ronn Starr, John Magruder, saxophones; Dave MacKay, piano and organ; Ray Neopolitan, Chuck Domanico, Frank De La Rosa, Vic Mio, basses; Steve Bohannon, Alan Estes, drums; Chino Baldes, conga drums.

The Charles Lloyd Quartet with Charles Lloyd, tenor saxophone; Keith Jarrett, piano; Cecil McBee, bass; Jack De Johnette, drums.

The John Handy Quintet, with John Handy, alto saxophone; Michael White, violin; Jerry Hahn, guitar; Don Thompson, bass; Terry Clarke, drums.

Gil Evans and the Monterey Jazz Festival All-Star Orchestra, presenting the World Premiere of a piece written and arranged by Gil Evans, commissioned by the Monterey Jazz Festival.

Sunday Evening, September 18, at 7:15 p.m. (early curtain):

The Randy Weston Sextet, with Randy Weston, piano; Cecil Payne, baritone saxophone; Ray Copeland, trumpet and flugelhorn; Bill Wood, bass; Lenny McBrowne, drums; Big Black, conga drums; guest star, Booker Ervin, tenor saxophone.

The Denny Zeitlin Trio with Denny Zeitlin, piano; Fred Marshall, bass; Jerry Granelli, drums.

Carmen McRae, vocalist, accompanied by the Norman Simmons Trio, with Norman Simmons, piano; Victor Sproles, bass; Frank Severino, drums.

Duke Ellington and his Famous Orchestra, with Edward Kennedy Ellington, leader, piano; Cootie Williams, Cat Anderson, Mercer Ellington, Herbie Jones, trumpets; Lawrence Brown, Charles Connors, Buster Cooper, trombones; Johnny Hodges, Russell Procope (clarinet), Paul Gonsalves, Jimmy Hamilton (clarinet), Harry Carney (clarinet), saxes; John Lamb, bass; Sam Woodyard, drums.

* * *

Charles Lloyd, 1966

It was a successful Festival, artistically, because people were peaking at Monterey. The Charles Lloyd Quartet would never be better. Butterfield and the Jefferson Airplane were stirring; Booker Ervin and Gerry Mulligan were wandering around as guest soloists. Gil Evans composed a special piece, and Count Basie and Duke Ellington were at the same Festival. And it was the year another big band was introduced. Lyons heard it at a club on Melrose, in Los Angeles. It was the most exciting band he'd heard since Kenton: Don Ellis and his loud, driving, crazy-new-rhythmed orchestra.

The introduction of Ellis and Keith Jarrett and Zawinul's "Mercy Mercy" would become milestones of the first 20 years.

Three records came out of this Festival: "Forest Flower" (Charles Lloyd) Atlantic, 1743.

"Bola Sete at the Monterey Jazz Festival," Verve v-8689.

"Don Ellis Orchestra Live at the Monterey Jazz Festival," Pacific Jazz, PJ-10112.

Conducting, Don Ellis style, 1966

Gil Evans rehearses the orchestra, 1966

Count Basie, 1966

The Jefferson Airplane, left to right: Jack Casady, Marty Balin, Jorma Kaukonen, Signe Anderson, Paul Kantner, 1966

1967

The tenth anniversary opened with a light and slide show. It opened with balloons and Don Ellis. It was the year the Festival reached to Europe and brought over Svend Asmussen, Jean-Luc Ponty, the Ambrosetti Quintet and Miljenko Prohaska. It was a foreshadowing of the next ten years.

The Festival was filmed. Jimmy Lyons was named chairman of the California Arts Commission (a jazz entrepreneur heading an arts commission!). Monterey audiences were just about half black and half white. No riots had broken out. It was a calm Pacific setting and the mood was reflected in the music.

The program opened at 8:30 p.m. on a Friday with a special 10th anniversary celebration in the arena. There followed:

The Dizzy Gillespie Quintet, with Jimmy Moody, sax and flute; Candy Finch, drums; Mike Longo, piano; Russell George, electric bass.

Illinois Jacquet, tenor saxophone; with Louis Bellson, drums; John Lewis, piano; and Ray Brown, bass.

The Don Ellis Orchestra.

And a Jazz Violin Conclave with Ray Nance, Svend Asmussen, Jean-Luc Ponty and others.

Saturday Afternoon, September 16, at 1:30 p.m.:

Genesis and Revelations.

The Clara Ward Singers.

T-Bone Walker, vocal and guitar.

B. B. King, vocal and guitar.

Richie Havens, vocal and guitar.

Big Brother and the Holding Company, with Peter Albin, bass, vocal; James Gurley, guitar, vocal; Sam Andrew, guitar, vocal; David Getz, drums; Janis Joplin, vocal.

Saturday Evening, September 16, at 8:15 p.m.:

The Woody Herman Orchestra with Mel Torme.

The Modern Jazz Quartet, with John Lewis, piano; Connie Kay, drums; Percy Heath, bass; Milt Jackson, vibes.

The Ambrosetti Quintet from Lugano, Switzerland, featuring bassist, Nils-Henning Orsted Pederson, with Flavio Ambrosetti, alto saxophone; Franco Ambrosetti, trumpet; George Gruntz, piano; Daniel Humair, drums.

Sunday Afternoon, September 17, at 1:30 p.m.:

The Don Ellis Orchestra, performing "Sketches" and "Memorial to Billy Strayhorn," by Louis Bellson.

The Gabor Szabo Quintet, with Gabor Szabo, guitar; Jimmy Stewart, guitar; Bill Goodwin, drums; Hal Gordon, conga drums; Lewis Kabok, bass.

The Ornette Coleman Quartet, with Ornette Coleman, alto saxophone, trumpet, violin; David Izenson, bass; Charles Haden, bass; Ed Blackwell, drums.

Gil Melle and the Electronic Jazz Quartet, with Gil Melle, Fred C. Stofflet, Forrest Westbrook and Ben Farel Matthews.

Miljenko Prohaska, conducting the Don Ellis Orchestra in a world premiere of a piece by Prohaska, commissioned by the Monterey Jazz Festival.

Sunday Evening, September 17, at 7:15 p.m. (early curtain):

The Dizzy Gillespie Quintet.

The Earl "Fatha" Hines Quartet, with Earl Hines, piano; Budd Johnson, saxophone; Oliver Jackson, drums; Bill Pemberton, bass.

Carmen McRae, vocal, accompanied by Norman Simmons.

The Woody Herman Orchestra, in a World Premiere of new music written for the Festival by Bill Holman.

*   *   *

There were commissions and sleeked-down sets. Groups were getting more expensive. Lyons was emphasizing new works, rather than endless programs. John Lewis was back as musical director, where he'd remain for the next ten years.

Earl "Fatha" Hines, 1967

T-Bone Walker and B.B. King, 1967

Woody Herman leads his Herd, 1967

Red Norvo, 1967

Larry Coryell, left, and Gary Burton, 1967

1968

Sam Smidt's slide show that opened last year's Festival was brought back to open this year's Festival. Ten years at Monterey: Coltrane and Mingus and Duke and Monk and Charles Lloyd and Basie and Gil Evans and Jack Teagarden and family and Ornette and Don Ellis and Jon Hendricks and Dizzy and Butterfield, Bloomfield and Janis Joplin and Carmen and Louis Armstrong and John Handy and Gerald Wilson and Miles, and all the aping and jamming and special compositions and guests at large, like Mulligan and John Lewis and Ray Brown and Benny Carter, and Desmond and Brubeck and Booker Ervin and Eric Dolphy and Wes Montgomery.

The Friday evening show was hosted by Mel Torme. It began at 9 p.m. (sharp as usual) with the Gary Burton Quartet, Gary Burton, vibes; Roy Haynes, drums; Steve Swallow, bass; Jerry Hahn, guitar.

And followed with:

The Oscar Peterson Trio, Oscar Peterson, piano; Sam Jones, bass; Louis Hayes, drums.

Mel Torme.

The Dektet, John Coppola, trumpet; Rudy Salvini, trumpet; Fred Mergy, trombone; Bob Tefft, French horn; Dick Douty, tuba; Rich Henry, alto saxophone; Tom Scott, tenor saxophone; Dave Madden, baritone saxophone; John Guerin, drums; Chuck Domanico, bass.

The Count Basie Orchestra, Count Basie, leader and piano; Gene Goe, Sonny Cohn, Al Aarons, Oscar Brashear, trumpets; Grover Mitchell, Steve Galloway, Richard Boone, Bill Hughes, trombones; Marshall Royal, Bobby Plater, Eddie "Lockjaw" Davis, Eric Dixon, Charles Fowlkes, saxophones; Freddie Green, guitar; Harold Jones, drums; Norman Keenan, bass; Malena Shaw, vocals.

Entr'acte: the Craig Hundley Trio, with Craig Hundley, piano; J.J. Wiggins, bass; Gary Chase, drums.

Saturday Afternoon, September 21, at 1:30 p.m.:

"Masters of the Blues."

The Vince Guaraldi Quartet, Vince Guaraldi, piano; Bobby Natenson, drums; Bob Maize, electric bass; Bob Addison, guitar. Featuring Mel Brown, special guest, guitar; Grady Tate, Festival debut, blues vocalist.

Jimmy Rushing.

Muddy Waters.

B.B. King.

"Big Mama" Willie Mae Thornton, accompanied by Harmonica George Smith, harmonica; Curtis Tilman, bass; Nat Dove, piano; Gus Wright, drums; B. Houston, guitar.

Saturday Evening, September 21, at 8:15 p.m.:

"An Evening with Carmen McRae," Carmen McRae, hostess.

The Gabor Szabo Quintet, Gabor Szabo, guitar; Jimmy Stewart, guitar; Lewis Kabok, bass; Dick Berk, drums; Hal Gordon, conga drums.

The Modern Jazz Quartet, John Lewis, piano and leader; Percy Heath, bass; Connie Kay, drums; Milt Jackson, vibes.

Carmen McRae, accompanied by Norman Simmons, piano; Percy Heath, bass; Connie Kay, drums; Francois Vos, guitar.

The Don Ellis Orchestra, Don Ellis, leader and trumpet; Glenn Stuart, Stu Blumberg, Bob Harmon, John Rosenberg, trumpets; Ernie Carlson, Glenn Ferris, Terry Woodson, trombones; Doug Bixby, tuba; Ron Starr, Frank Strozier, Sam Falzone, John Klemmer, John Magruder, woodwinds; Pete Robinson, piano; Ray Neapolitan, Dave Parlato, basses; Ralph Humphrey, drums; Gene Strimling, percussion; Lee Pastora, conga drums.

Entr'acte: The Third Wave, Georgiana, Regina, Jamie, Stephanie and Jody Ente, with the George Duke Trio, George Duke, piano; John Heard, bass; Al Cecchi, drums. (George Duke, a young musician in the Bay Area, would come back ten years later and blow everyone out of their seats.)

Sunday Afternoon, September 22, at 1:30 p.m.:

"All Strung Out."

The Gabor Szabo Quintet, with special guests, Bill Plummer, sitar and Mike White, violin.

"A Generation of Vibers," with Gary Burton, Bobby Hutcherson, Cal Tjader, Red Norvo, and Milt Jackson, accompanied by the Modern Jazz Quartet.

"Jazz Suite on the Mass Texts," Lalo Schifrin with Orchestra and Choir, featuring Tom Scott, saxophone, in the debut of Schifrin's "Jazz Suite." Lalo Schifrin, conductor; John Coppola, Larry Souza, trumpets; Fred Mergy, Gordon Messick, trombones; Bob Tefft, French horn; Dick Douty, tuba; Jack Van Der Wyk, John Rae, Tony Cirone, Lynn Blessing, percussion; Joe Andres, Melanie Rogers, harps; John Guerin, drums; Chuck Domanico, bass; Mike Lang, piano; chorus under the direction of Joseph Liebling.

Sunday Evening, September 22, at 7:15 p.m. (early curtain):

"An Evening with Mr. B" (Billy Eckstine), and the first annual outing of the "Fatha" Hines Distinguished Alumni Association.

Billy Eckstine — host.

The Cal Tjader Quintet, with Cal Tjader, vibes; James McCabe, bass; Al Zulaica, piano; John Rae, drums; Armando Perazza, conga drums.

The Tom Scott Quartet, Tom Scott, saxophone; John Guerin, drums; Chuck Domanico, bass; Mike Lang, piano.

Billy Eckstine.

The Earl "Fatha" Hines Orchestra, Earl Hines, leader and piano; John Coppola, Rudy Salvini, Zane Woodworth, Bob Mitchell, trumpets; Fred Mergy, Jack Sava, Bruce Wolff, Gordon Messick, trombones; Rich Henry, Chuck Peterson, Bill Perkins, Budd Johnson, Curtis Lowe, saxophones; Oliver Jackson, drums; Milan Rezabek, bass.

The Earl "Fatha" Hines Quartet, Earl Hines, piano; Budd Johnson, tenor saxophone; Oliver Jackson, drums; Milan Rezabek, bass.

The Dizzy Gillespie Quintet, Dizzy Gillespie, trumpet; James Moody, saxophone; Paul West, bass; Mike Longo, piano; Candy Finch, drums.

Entr'acte: Palinho Quartet, Palinho, percussion; Lenita Bruno, vocal; Chaim LeBak, piano; Perry Steinberg, bass.

* * *

Jimmy Rushing's at Monterey, and everything's fine, 1970

The Sunday night program was old, but it swung. Billy Eckstine and Earl Hines together. There wasn't really anything new at the Festival. Tom Scott, an L.A. studio musician, and John Klemmer, with the Don Ellis orchestra, would go on to establish names for themselves. But nobody represented the expressionistic movement in jazz.

Oscar Peterson, 1971

Left to right: James Moody, Dizzy Gillespie, Paul West, playing at the 1963 Festival

1969

This was the year of the Tipalet Experience. A little cigar, flavored in cherry, natural, burgundy and wild blueberry, was handed out at the gates. Muriel sponsored a piece of the Festival. The whole green reeked of these five-for-25-cents bitted smokes. Their ad campaign was "blow in her face and she'll follow you anywhere." Even at Monterey, where by Sunday night men and women are chasing each other up trees, you couldn't pick anyone up by blowing cigar smoke in their face.

The program started on Friday evening, at 9 p.m.:

The Peanuts Hucko-Red Norvo Quintet, Peanuts Hucko, clarinet; Red Norvo, vibes; Morey Feld, drums; Louise Tobin, vocals; David McKenna, piano; Bill Bastien, bass.

The Modern Jazz Quartet, John Lewis, piano; Percy Heath, bass; Connie Kay, drums; Milt Jackson, vibes; with Jean-Luc Ponty, violin, guest artist.

Tony Williams Lifetime, Tony Williams, percussion; Larry Young, organ; John McLaughlin, electric guitar.

Sly and the Family Stone, Sly Stone, vocals and leader; Freddie Stone, vocals and guitar; Larry Graham, vocals and bass; Gregg Errico, drums; Jerry Martin, saxophone; Rosie Stone, piano, organ and vocals; Cynthia Robinson, trumpet.

Saturday Afternoon, September 20, at 1:30 p.m.:

Bobby Bryant and the Monterey Jazz Festival Soul All-Stars, featuring Little Esther Phillips, vocals. All-Stars: Bobby Bryant, leader and trumpet; Buddy Childers, Paul Hubinon, Freddie Hill, Reunald Jones, Jr., trumpets; Mike Wimberly, Lou Blackburn, Fred Morrell, George Bohanon, trombones; Ernie Watts, Herman Riley, Peter Christlieb, saxophones; Mel Moore, violin; Dwight Carver, French horn; Don Waldrup, tuba; Mike Anthony, guitar; Joe Sample, piano; John Duke, bass; Wilton Felder, Fender bass; John Guerin, drums; Bob Norris, conga drums.

Willie "The Lion" Smith.

Roberta Flack and her Trio, Roberta Flack, vocals and piano; Bernard Sweetney, drums;

Marshall Hawkins, bass. (Roberta Flack went over so well, she played an unscheduled set in the Saturday evening concert. It was a song-for-song duplicate of this set.)

Buddy Guy and his Blues Band, Buddy Guy, guitar, vocals; Phillip Guy, guitar; Ernest Johnson, bass; Jessie Jackson, drums; A.C. Reed, horn.

The Lighthouse, with Skip Prokop, leader, drums and vocals; Paul Hoffert, musical director, keyboards, vibes; Ralph Cole, guitar and vocals; Grant Fullerton, bass and vocals; Pinky Dauvin, percussion and vocals; Ian Guenther, violin; Don Dinovo, violin and viola; Don Whitton, cello; Leslie Schneider, cello; Freddy Stone, trumpet and flugel; Arnie Chycoski, trumpet and flugel; Howard Shore, alto saxophone; Russ Little, trombone.

Saturday Evening, September 20, at 8:15 p.m.:

Bobby Bryant and the Monterey Jazz Festival Soul All-Stars.

The Miles Davis Quintet, Miles Davis, trumpet; Dave Holland, bass; Chick Corea, electric piano; Wayne Shorter, tenor and soprano sax; Jack DeJohnette, drums.

Joe Williams, accompanied by Ellis Larkins, piano; John Heard, bass; Alan Cecchi, drums.

The Thelonious Monk Quartet, with Thelonious Monk, piano; Charles Rouse, tenor saxophone; John Guerin, drums; Chuck Berghofer, bass.

(Monk also played music arranged by Oliver Nelson, with the Festival All-Stars.)

Entr'acte: Monty Alexander, piano; John Heard, bass; Alan Cecchi, drums.

Sunday Afternoon, September 21, at 1:30 p.m.: "Strings for Monterey."

Jean-Luc Ponty, violin, with Bobby Bryant and the Monterey Jazz Festival Orchestra in premiere performances of: "81," by Ron Carter; "Waltz for Clara," by Ponty; "Hipo Mode Del-Sol," by Ponty; and "The Loner," by Cedar Walton.

Josef Zawinul, piano, with Bill Fischer conducting the Festival Orchestra in the World Premiere of "Rise and Fall of the Third Wave," by Bill Fischer.

Nat Adderley, cornet, with Bill Fischer and the Orchestra: "Biafra," by Nat Adderley; "Nobody Knows," by Fischer.

The Modern Jazz Quartet and the Los Angeles String Quartet, Paul Shure and Bonnie Douglas, violins; Douglas Davis, cello; Peter Mark, viola.

World Premiere of compositions and arrangements by John Lewis: "Dido's Lament," adapted from Purcell's opera, "Dido and Aeneas"; "Vendome," by Lewis; "Aria from the Suite in D Major," by J.S. Bach, arranged by Lewis; and "Sketch" and "Alexander's Fugue," by Lewis.

"Progression in Tempo," by Gunther Schuller.

The Fourth Way, with Michael White, violin; Mike Nock, piano; Ron McClure, bass; Eddie Marshall, percussion.

(And a huge jam session, called "Improvisations for Sunday.")

Sunday Evening, September 21, at 7:15 p.m.:

The Buddy Rich Band, Buddy Rich, leader and drums; Mike Price, John DeFlon, Kenny Faulk, George Zonce, trumpets; Rick Stepton, Vince Diaz, Don Switzer, trombones; Win Davis, Richie Cole, Pat La Barbera, Don Englert, Joe Calo, saxophones; Dave Lahm, piano and organ; Bob Magnusson, bass and Fender bass.

The Cannonball Adderley Quintet, with Julian "Cannonball" Adderley, leader and saxophones; Nat Adderley, cornet; Joe Zawinul, piano; Roy McCurdy, drums; Walter Booker, bass.

Sarah Vaughan, accompanied by John Veith, piano; Ed Pucci, drums; Gus Mancuso, bass.

Jean-Luc Ponty, violin, with George Duke, piano; Alan Cecchi, drums; John Heard, bass.

* * *

The Festival was an odd combination of pop and serious. Little Esther Phillips and Sly and the Family Stone and Roberta Flack and a sophisticated rock group from Canada, the Lighthouse. And all the serious, John Lewis-inspired European music by Schuller and Jean-Luc Ponty and the MJQ.

It was a Festival that featured Miles Davis groping for a new sound. He'd eventually find it ("Bitches Brew") but this audience was impatient with his long, anxious noodlings.

On Sunday night the juice went out on Sarah Vaughan. She just kept singing: "Can someone fix this goddam no good mike?"

Sarah Vaughan

Left to right: Miles Davis, Dave Holland, Wayne Shorter, 1969

Sly Stone, 1969

Thelonious Monk, 1969

You don't have to be on stage, or on the program, to be part of the show at Monterey. The audience loves to get into the act, playing, dancing, showing off their style (1969).

1970

Besides having Dizzy Gillespie as this year's roving ambassador (old Monterey), there was new Monterey: youth concerts. Youth concerts would eventually become the high point of the Festival.

The Jazz Festival had already given grants and supported high school and college music programs. Now it was going to start bringing young musicians to the September fairgrounds.

The Festival started on Friday with Tim Weisberg. Lyons had met Weisberg in a L.A. office and Weisberg agreed to play the Festival if he could be introduced to Duke Ellington. They ended up playing on the same program.

Friday Evening, September 18, at 9 p.m.:
The Tim Weisberg Quintet, with Tim Weisberg, flute; Lynn Blessing, vibes; Mel Telford, drums; Art Johnson, guitar; Dave Parlato, bass.

The Modern Jazz Quartet, John Lewis, piano; Percy Heath, bass; Connie Kay, drums; Milt Jackson, vibes.

The Alan Copeland Singers, with the MJQ. Voices: Alan Copeland, Susan Talman, Beverly Kelly, Ginny Mancini, Sue Allen, Chuck Kelly, Tom Kenny, Bill Brown.

The Duke Ellington Orchestra, premiering a new work: "The Afro-Eurasian Eclipse," by Ellington. Duke Ellington, leader and piano; Chuck Conners, Mitchell Wood, Malcolm Taylor, trombones; Cat Anderson, Mercer Ellington, Fred Stone, Cootie Williams, trumpets; Paul Gonsalves, Harold Ashby, Norris Turney, Russell Procope, Harry Carney, saxophones; Rufus Jones, drums; Wild Bill Davis, organ; Joe Benjamin, bass; Tony Watkins, vocals.

Saturday Afternoon, September 19, at 1:30 p.m.:

The Johnny Otis Show, featuring the Rhythm and Blues Hall of Fame All-Stars, Johnny Otis, master of ceremonies, with Jimmy Rushing, Big Joe Turner, Ivory Joe Hunter, Charles Brown, Roy Milton, Eddie "Cleanhead" Vinson, Roy Brown, Pee Wee Crayton, "Sugarcane" Harris, Delmar "Mighty Mouth" Evans, Margie Evans.

Introducing "Shuggie" Otis. Special guest star, Little Esther Phillips. Plus, Gene "The Mighty Flea" Connors, trombone; Jim Wynn, Richard Aplenalt, Clifford Solomon, Preston Love, saxophones; Melvin Moore, trumpet; Paul Lagos, drums; Jim Bradshaw, guitar; Lawrence "Slim" Dickens, bass.

(T-Bone Walker, scheduled to be with the show, was ill.)

Saturday Evening, September 19, at 8:15 p.m.:
Slim and Slam: Slim Gaillard, guitar and vocals; Slam Stewart, bass; Milt Buckner, piano; Jo Jones, drums.

Joe Williams, accompanied by Ellis Larkins, piano; and the Woody Herman Orchestra.

The Cannonball Adderley Quintet, Cannonball Adderley, alto saxophone; Nat Adderley, cornet; Joe Zawinul, piano; Roy McCurdy, drums; Walter Booker, bass.

The Woody Herman Orchestra, Woody Herman, leader, alto saxophone, clarinet and vocals; Rig Powell, Forrest Buchtel, Tony Klatka, Tom Harrell, Bill Byrne, trumpets; Ira Nepus, Kurt Berg, Lutten Taylor, trombones; Frank Tiberi, Steve Lederer, Mike Morris, Ed Xiques, saxophones; Alan Broadbent, piano; Tom Azzerelo, Fender bass; Ed Soph, drums.

Sunday Afternoon, September 20, at 1:30 p.m.:
The Oakland Youth Chamber Orchestra, under the direction of Denis deCoteau.

The Modern Jazz Quartet, augmented by the Oakland Youth Chamber Orchestra, in works by John Lewis, Miljenko Prohaska and Joaquin Rodrigo.

The Bill Evans Trio, Bill Evans piano; Marty Morrell, drums; Eddie Gomez, bass. And the Trio plus Chamber Orchestra in works by Bill Evans.

Prince Lasha's Firebirds, Prince Lasha and Sonny Simmons, saxophones; Buster Williams, bass; Charles Moffett, drums; Bobby Hutcherson, vibes.

The Cannonball Adderley Quintet and Oakland Youth Chamber Orchestra in two presentations: "Tensity," composed and conducted by David Axelrod, and "Experience in E" by William Fischer and Josef Zawinul, conducted by Mr. Fischer.

Bill Evans, 1975

Gabor Szabo and the Oakland Youth Chamber Orchestra in the World Premiere of "Circle Suite" by William Fischer. Mr. Fischer conducting.

The Oakland Youth Chamber Orchestra: Peter Maunu, Kati Kyme, Kristin Keddington, Jerilyn Jorgenson, Jamie Jan, Marianne Votto, Vickie Walters, Ann Lyness, Peter Jaffee, Christine Bury, Jo Anne Wingert, Laurie Goren, Wendy Foster, Lynn McCarty, violins; Betsy London, Kazi Pitelka, Lynne Morrow, Alison Dunn, Lorrie Hunt, Jackie Chew, violas; Garfield Moore, Amy Radnor, Joel Cohen, Heidi Jacob, Kari Lindstedt, Dan Greenspan, cellos; Charles Couchot, Robert Gay, Carla Lemon, basses; Diane Wang, Angela Koregelos, flutes and piccolo; Ralph Hassman, Stephen Gancher, oboe and English horn; Alex Foster, Oliver Miller, clarinets; Mark Forry, Bernard Norris, Kent James, bassoons; Kurt Ingram, Diana Bowman, Ken Weisner, Brian McCarty, French horns; Jeff Micheli, Bert Truax, Eric Nelson, trumpets; Mike Basta, Allen Sanders, Phil Herring, trombones; Kazi Pitelka, tuba; Lydia Moshkin, Chris Braun, Kim Venaas, percussion.

Sunday Evening, September 20, at 7:15 p.m. (early curtain):

The Gabor Szabo Sextet, Gabor Szabo, guitar; Felix Falcon, congas; Wolfgang Meltz, Fender bass; John Dentz, drums; Lynn Blessing, vibes; Sandra Crouch, tambourine.

Leon Thomas and Black Lightning, Leon Thomas, vocals; Sonny Morgan, Afro-percussion and flute; James Spaulding, saxophone and flute; Arthur Sterling, piano and miscellaneous instruments; Richie Landrum, Afro-percussion; Raphael Garrett, bass; Arthur "Sharkie" Lewis, drums.

The Hampton Hawes Trio, Hampton Hawes, piano; Leroy Vinnegar, bass; Donald Bailey, drums.

Sonny Stitt and Gene Ammons, saxophones, plus the Hampton Hawes Trio.

The Buddy Rich Orchestra.

Duke Ellington, guest master of ceremonies.

       ✲   ✲   ✲

The place was hysterical for Slim and Slam. Lyons found Slam teaching in Buffalo and Slim in Los Angeles. They hadn't sung and played together in years. They sang their odd, goofball lyrics and Dizzy's ("you wouldn't throw a dying sow an acorn, a crippled crab a crutch, baby you ain't so much a much"), and the good time Saturday evening audience was in heaven.

It was a Festival of diversities: Johnny Otis and his fantastic blues show, which was recorded here ("The Johnny Otis Show Live at Monterey," Epic EG-30473), came up from Los Angeles and filled the whole easy-going Saturday afternoon program. The serious Sunday afternoon affair centered around a youth orchestra and its director, deCoteau, a young black man who had gone to join the Miami symphony some years earlier: he was hired by tape; when they saw his color, they gave him a year and got rid of him.

There was new music represented by Prince Lasha and Leon Thomas. Bill Evans made his debut. Gene Ammons and Hampton Hawes debuted, both just coming out of prison on drug charges. Duke Ellington was gracing the stage as emcee and musician. The direction for the seventies was clear for Lyons: school jazz.

Dizzy Gillespie and Duke Ellington, 1970

Gene Ammons, left, and Sonny Stitt, 1970

Monterey means jazz in the open air and relaxation on the sunny fairgrounds between shows (1969)

1971

The Festival was dedicated to Louis Armstrong (1900-1971). He had been at Monterey from the beginning, blowing and singing, and kept on coming back, his eyesight and health fading.

A nursery in Ontario, California, which named a new rose Jazz Fest, sponsored part of the Festival and shipped rows and rows of these new roses to Monterey. The name of the nursery: Armstrong.

Many old names were back this year. Mulligan and Brubeck and Louie Bellson and Carmen McRae and John Handy. The Festival was having less of those bewildering wonderful moments.

The music was okay, most of it pat, good jazz, lots of okay jamming. The people were regulars, and their music wasn't surprising anyone.

Lyons didn't go for experimental jazz. He grew but he grew another way. He went for high school kids. The Festival sponsored California high school jazz competitions and put together an all-star band.

Sunday afternoons, which used to be reserved for Monterey experimental music, now belonged to the kids. Audiences were small and bored. Who wanted to see kids playing standards?

By 1977 the kids would be the highlight of the Festival.

Monterey 1971 started off on a Friday evening with the Dave Brubeck Quartet, Dave Brubeck, piano; Gerry Mulligan, baritone saxophone; Alan Dawson, drums; Jack Six, bass.

And followed with:

Miss Carmen McRae, accompanied by Nat Pierce, piano.

The Louie Bellson All-Star Band, with Chuck Findley, Harry Edison, Sal Marquez, Conte Candoli, trumpets; Bill Tole, Nick DiMaio, Carl Fontana, Kenny Schroyer, trombones; Joe Romano, Ray Pizzi, Pete Christlieb, Don Menza, Allan Beutler, saxophones; Joe Pass, Ray Brown, Bill Sloan, Jack Arnold, Louie Bellson, rhythm.

Saturday Afternoon, September 18, at 1:30 p.m.:

"Kansas City Revisited."

The Jesse Price Blues Band, featuring Big Joe Turner. Jesse Price, drums; Billy Hadnott, bass; Chester Lane, piano; Harry "Sweets" Edison, trumpet; Jimmy Forrest, tenor saxophone; Preston Love, alto saxophone; Wallace Huff, trombone.

Mary Lou Williams.

Jay McShann's Kansas City Six, Jay McShann, piano; Paul Gunther, drums; Billy Hadnott, bass; Herman Bell, tenor saxophone and guitar; Claude Williams, violin; Harry "Sweets" Edison, trumpet.

Al Hibbler.

Saturday Evening, September 18, at 8:15 p.m.:

Erroll Garner, accompanied by Jose Mangual, conga drums; Jimmie Smith, percussion; Ernest McCarty, Jr., bass.

Improvisations by John Handy, alto saxophone; Ali Akbar Khan, sarod; Zakir Hussain, tabla; accompanied by Susan Rosenblum and Alvina Quintana, tambouras.

Jimmy Witherspoon and friends.

The Thad Jones-Mel Lewis Band, featuring Bobby Brookmeyer, trombone; Marvin Stamm, trumpet; Richard Davis, bass; Roland Hanna, piano; Jerome Richardson, saxophone; Dee Dee Bridgewater, vocals.

Sunday Afternoon, September 19, at 1:30 p.m.:

"Jazz Today and Tomorrow."

The Ygnacio Valley High School Jazz Band (winner of the First California High School Jazz Band Competition). Mary Fettig, Linda Pennington, Kent James, Scott Sanford, Mike Flaherty, Dave Sweeney, saxophones; Gary Smith, Kris Bowerman, Bob Fernbach, Rich Fernbach, Dave Langelier, trombones; Dave Grover, Marc Langelier, Wes Taylor, Damon Dillon, Hank Davis, Bill Charlesworth, Keith Wilson, trumpets; Dave de Marche, Paul Larimer, Neil Finn, percussion; Mark Phillips, electric bass; Andy Knox, string bass; Tom Charlesworth, piano; Bill Burke, director.

The California All-Star High School Jazz Band, conducted by Oliver Nelson, Ladd McIntosh and Mundell Lowe, in special performances of works by the three conductors. The presentation featured guest soloists: Clark Terry, trumpet; Louie Bellson, drums; Ray Brown, bass; John Handy, alto saxophone. Additional soloists featured were Albert Wing, saxophone; Stu Goldberg, piano; Walter Fowler, trumpet.

The All-Star Band: Jeff Micheli, Larry Machado, Kevin Wilde, Mike Weatherwax, Eric Nelson, trumpets; Dean Hubbard, Jack Erb, Rob Katibah, Rich Carson, Andy Goldstein, trombones; Rick Condit, Ed Ferrero, Gary Mendonca, Ray Griffen, Dave Deichman, saxophones; Steve De Patie, piano; Dave Moreno, bass; Tom McCray, drums; Barry Coates, guitar; Chris Braun, vibes.

The McMinnville Oregon Twilighters. Voices: Sharon Cross, Charyle Mather, Karen Rose, Coleene Sanders, Diane Shipman, Sue Swenson, Kathy Yonker, Aileene Cline, Lindy Leonnig, Bonnie McLane, Sara Steele, Connie Gottel, Scott Copeland, Jerry Gross, Dave New, Jeff Standy, Stan Yankee, Steve Blaka, Dick Jones, Nat Kerr, Peter Mead, John Rathkey, Paul Paddock, Kris Dunn, Robert Dickson. Under the direction of Doug Anderson.

Sunday Evening, September 19, at 7:15 p.m. (early curtain):

"A Salute to Jazz at the Philharmonic," with a special tribute to its founder, Norman Granz.

The Oscar Peterson Trio, Oscar Peterson, piano; Louis Hayes, drums; Nils-Henning Orsted Pedersen, bass.

Miss Sarah Vaughan.

The Jam Session: Oscar Peterson, piano; Zoot Sims, Eddie "Lockjaw" Davis, tenor saxophones; Benny Carter, alto saxophone; Clark Terry, trumpet; Bill Harris, trombone; Louie Bellson, drums; Ray Brown, bass.

*   *   *

Norman Granz had been a big influence on Jimmy Lyons. That style of big name jam session was what Monterey was all about. Lyons and Granz had worked together 30 years before, when Lyons was doing armed forces radio. Now Granz and John Lewis were good friends. They were neighbors in southern France. They went on gourmet eating binges together.

Dizzy Gillespie was roving ambassador again this year. There were four, at least, fine pianists—Oscar Peterson, Erroll Garner, Jay McShane and Mary Lou Williams.

But it was the kids that brought out the father in Lyons. They melted him. Perhaps the old L.A. and N.Y. warhorses were too jaded. The kids could play the same old tunes and make them seem young. It would take a long time, though, before the audiences would hear that. They still wanted the big names.

Oscar Peterson backed by Louis Hayes, drums, and Nils-Henning Orsted Pedersen, 1971

Louie Bellson, left, and Joe Pass, 1971

Roy Eldridge, center, soloing with, left to right, Clark Terry, Zoot Sims, Eddie "Lockjaw" Davis, Mundell Lowe, 1971

1972

This was the year Toots Thielmans, a small Belgian harmonica player, would get the biggest standing ovation in Monterey history with a version of "The Man I Love," with the Quincy Jones Orchestra.

It was also the year Dizzy Gillespie crammed in Monterey between Midwest concerts, being driven like a madman from a concert in Indiana to a plane in Illinois, just to appear at Monterey. Dizzy and Monterey were becoming one. Why him again, people asked. Why not some of the other trumpet players around? Why not Freddie Hubbard or Lester Bowie? Because, Lyons would say, he's the best. Not only that, Lyons understood Dizzy. He didn't understand some of the modern trumpet players. Dizzy is warm and open, and doesn't care whether you're black or white. He plays music, not politics. And Lyons loved him for being a great entertainer and a great human being.

Buddy Rich sat in for Stan Kenton this year, when Kenton couldn't appear to lead his own band. Rich had made a strange offer. He said he'd play at Monterey for hotel room and cartage just so he could test out his healing broken foot. It was strange because Lyons and Rich had had a run-in at another concert Lyons had booked. It was eventually cleared up; both men's feelings hurt. This was in Orange County at a festival that Rich had been late in playing. When Lyons pressed Rich about starting time, Rich threatened to pound Lyons. Now they were doing each other this bizarre favor. Lyons would get his big name and Rich would get his foot working. Jazz, after all, is a very small world and grudges tend to dissipate in the ever-shrinking space.

The program started on Friday evening with the Modern Jazz Quartet, John Lewis, piano; Percy Heath, bass; Connie Kay, drums; and Milt Jackson, vibraphone; with special guests Laurindo Almeida and George Benson, guitars.

And there followed:

Elvin Jones Quartet, Elvin Jones, drums; Gene Perla, bass; David Liebman and Steve Grossman, saxophones.

Stan Kenton and his Orchestra, Stan Kenton, piano; featuring Nat Pierce and Buddy Rich, with Jay Saunders, Dennis Noday, Mike Vax, Mike Snustead, Ray Brown, trumpets; Dick Shearer, Fred Carter, Harvey Coonan, Mike Wallace, Phil Herring, trombones; Quin Davis, Richard Torres, Chris Galuman, Chuck Carter, Willie Maiden, saxophones; Peter Erskine, drums; Ramon Lopez, conga drums; John Worster, bass.

Saturday Afternoon, September 16, at 1:30 p.m.:

"Evolution of the Blues Song" with Jon Hendricks, composer and narrator; with Bessie Griffin, Eddie "Cleanhead" Vinson, Jimmy Witherspoon, and the Seaside Community Choir (a local choir). (This was an attempt to recreate the exciting show of 1961, something that never really could be recreated.)

Saturday Evening, September 16, at 8:15 p.m.:

Herbie Hancock Septet, Herbie Hancock, piano; Eddie Henderson, trumpet and fluegelhorn; Benny Maupin, alto flute, bass clarinet, and saxophone; Julian Priester, trombone; Charles "Buster" Williams, bass; Billy Hart, drums and percussion; Pat Gleeson, Moog Synthesizer.

Sonny Rollins Quartet, Sonny Rollins, saxophone; George Cables, piano; Henry Franklin, bass; Dave Lee, drums.

Joe Williams with John Lewis, piano; Ron Carter, bass; Louie Bellson, drums; Mundell Lowe, guitar.

Mary Lou Williams Trio, Mary Lou Williams, piano; Milt Suggs, bass; Louie Bellson, drums.

The Giants of Jazz (a salute to Norman Granz' concept of Jazz at the Philharmonic), with Art Blakey, drums; Roy Eldridge, trumpet; Al McKibbon, bass; Thelonious Monk, piano; Sonny Stitt, saxophone; Clark Terry, trumpet; Kai Winding, trombone.

Sunday Afternoon, September 17, at 1:30 p.m.:

Bonita High School Band, with Gordon Goodwin, Kevin Sly, Delbert Hillary, Julie Bathke, Jeff Beer, saxophones; Mia Kinsinger, flute; Gregg Hook, Kevin Mason, Mark Goodwin, Randy Guck, Jay Nichols, Mike Morales, Robbie Davis, trumpets; Bill Synder, Eric Olsen, Tom Slanker, Bruce NcNaught, Bill Bowers, trombones; John Tec, tuba; Steve Hawk, bass; Joe Movich, Larry Cornwell, guitars; Ron Schrock, Scott Magallanes, Eddie Flanders, David Cathers, Ken Wedin, rhythm percussion.

Alain Locke School Jazz Combo, with Gerald Brown, bass; Dathan Dedman, trumpet; Rai Harris, tenor saxophone; Glenn Jeffery, guitar; Lamidas Mack, trombone; Patrice Rushen, piano; Fritz Wise, drums.

Louie Bellson, Roy Burns, Ron Carter, John Lewis, Mundell Lowe, Ladd McIntosh, Oliver Nelson and Clark Terry, featured with the All-Star California High School Jazz Band: Bill Theurer, Rick Bezouska, Daryl Gest, Chuck Bumcrot, Dathan Dedman, trumpets; Chris Gillock, Steve Tyler, Kent Dunavent, Ed Hull, Rick Hage, trombones; Chuck Hansen, David Hlebo, Lynn Askew, Gary Mendonca, Don Gardner, saxophones; Patrice Rushen, piano; Gerald Brown, bass; Sheldon Mann, James Liptak, drums; Glenn Jeffery, guitar.

Sunday Evening, September 17, at 7:15 p.m. (early curtain):

Roberta Flack, piano and vocal, with Eric Gale, guitar; Richard Tee, electric piano; Ralph McDonald, percussion; Terry Plumieri, bass; Chuck Rainey, Fender bass; Rick Marotta, drums.

Quincy Jones Band, with Bobby Bryant, Buddy Childers, Oscar Brashear, Albert Aarons, trumpets; James Cleveland, Frank Rosolino, Benny Powell, Maurice Spears, trombones; Sidney Muldrow, French horn; Jerome Richardson, Peter Christlieb, Fred Jackson, Ernie Watts, Bill Green, saxophones; Ray Brown, bass; Chuck Rainey, Fender bass; Grady Tate, drums; Mike Woffard, piano; Toots Thielmans, harmonica; Tommy Johnson, tuba; Marti McCall, Geraldine Jones, Petesey Powell, vocalists.

Cal Tjader Quintet, with Cal Tjader, vibes; Mike Wolff, piano; Dick Berk, drums; John Heard, bass; Michael Smithe, congas; and guests, Willie Bobo, timbales, and Dizzy Gillespie, trumpet.

* * *

Herbie Hancock

As soon as Dizzy walks on a stage the audience goes wild. Late Sunday night, when the Latin jam started, people were dancing in the aisles.

The rest of the Festival seemed flat, even though the high school afternoons were beginning to reap talent. Mary Fettig, who played last year, went on to join Kenton, and Patrice Rushen who played piano this year, would go on to be a star.

Roberta Flack and Quincy Jones, starting their rise on pop charts, were costly, but the audiences liked them.

Herbie Hancock made it through half a number. This was the kind of music Lyons detests. Noodling avant garde.

The high school kids were appreciative, swinging and playing hard. Most of the kids came from upper class suburbs. You would think they would come from deprived ghettos. But those parents that can afford to give their kids lessons watch their kids win competitions. It's like anything else. Playing a saxophone well is not magic. It's work, diligence, and often a good teacher and a driving parent.

Quincy Jones, left, and Toots Thielmans, 1972

"The Evolution of the Blues Song;" Jon Hendricks and the Seaside Community Choir, 1972

Eddie "Cleanhead" Vinson, 1970

Ladd McIntosh conducts the California All-Star High School Jazz Band, 1972   127

1973

Even with the limits Monterey was setting for itself, the Festival could shine. On Saturday afternoon, four elderly gentlemen walked out on stage and danced their hearts out. Baby Lawrence, Buster Brown, Chuck Green and John T. McPhee showed what music looks like when you tap it out.

On Friday night the Pointer Sisters, a couple of years before they would become stars, camped their way up and down the stage. The weird thing about the Pointer Sisters is that they look like jazz in the '40s; they look like Cotton Club devotees. They were all in their 20s and their father was a preacher in Oakland, but every day, off stage or on, they dressed in these second-hand, thirty-year-old clothes. Later, second-hand fashions would become chic.

On Sunday night, theme night, Lyons brought out families. Thad and Elvin Jones, the Heath brothers, among others, and Jimmy Rowles with his daughter Stacy.

The program on Friday evening started with Clare Fischer behind a white plastic keyboard, a Yamaha EX-42. He was accompanied by Gary Foster and Pete Christlieb, reeds; Jim Hughart, bass; Larry Bunker, percussion.

There followed a piano playhouse, with Ellis Larkins, Billy Taylor, Toshiko Akiyoshi, John Lewis, pianos; Ray Brown, bass; Mundell Lowe, guitar; Roy Burns, drums.

The Pointer Sisters, Bonnie, June, Anita and Ruth, with Norman Landsberg, piano; John Noonan, bass; Gaylord Burke, drums.

Buddy Rich and his Orchestra.

Saturday Afternoon, September 22, at 1:30 p.m.:
"Singin' the Blues."
Jimmy Rogers and his Chicago Blues Band, Jimmy Rogers, guitar and vocals; Fred Below, drums; Louis Meyer, guitar; Dave Meyer, bass; Bob Reed, piano; Freddie King, guitar.
Mance Lipscomb.

Dave Alexander Trio, Dave Alexander, piano; Smiley Winters, drums; Peggy Mitchell, bass.
Eddie "Cleanhead" Vinson.
Bo Diddley.
History of the Jazz Dance, with Baby Lawrence, Buster Brown, Chuck Green, John T. McPhee.
Jon Hendricks, host and Master of Ceremonies.
(Years ago Monterey began bringing people out of retirement or obscurity. Helen Humes, Jimmy Witherspoon . . . and this year Jimmy Rogers. Rogers had been a prolific songwriter and had worked the blues circuit around Chicago and the Midwest. The past few years he had been driving a cab in Chicago.)
(Dave Alexander, then a smoker and drinker, has since given up both and changed his name to Omar Khayyam. He still works the Bay Area, as a single and in small groups.)

Saturday Evening, September 22, at 8:15 p.m.:
"Bird Night."
Dizzy Gillespie and his Quintet, with Dizzy Gillespie, trumpet; Mickey Roker, drums; Earl May, bass; Mike Longo, piano; Al Gafa, guitar.
Modern Jazz Quartet, John Lewis, piano; Percy Heath, bass; Connie Kay, drums; Milt Jackson, vibes.
Carmen McRae.
Supersax (a group of Los Angeles studio musicians who put Charlie Parker's solos into ensemble transcriptions), Jack Nimitz, baritone sax; Warne Marsh and Jay Migliori, tenor sax; Joe Lopes and Med Flory, alto sax; Conte Candoli, trumpet; Buddy Clark, bass; Ronnell Bright, piano; Jake Hanna, drums.
A special tribute to Charlie "Bird" Parker featuring Dizzy Gillespie, Max Roach, John Lewis, Milt Jackson, Ray Brown, Sonny Stitt, Frank Rosolino.

Sunday Afternoon, September 23, at 1:30 p.m.:
Jazz Stars of Today and Tomorrow.
Corona High School Jazz Band: Eric Norland, Jeff Ward, Mike Ernst, Mark Hornberger, Mike Wuflestad, trumpets; Verne Holmwood, Mike Danner, Steve Holtman, Vernon Whitt, Steve

Paulson, trombones; Greg Huckins, Paul Pettit, Dave Hlebo, Doug Flynn, Rob Trantow, saxophones; Steve Dahl, piano; Wade Lachman, bass; Pat Wilson, Blake Gardner, Jim Dell, guitar.

Grant Union High School Jazz Combo, Darryl Howard, trombone; Ed Simental, tenor sax; Dennis Adams, drums; Joe Espinoza, alto sax; Mike Brookins, bass; Leon Garner, piano; Jerome Thornton, conga drum and percussion.

California All-Star High School Jazz Band, Chuck Howe, Chuck Bumcrot, Bill Greene, Mike Miller, Stacy Rowles, trumpets; Bill Snyder, Jack Erb, Brian Taylor, Kris Bowerman, Joe Fields, trombones; Doug Rinaldo and Gordon Goodwin, alto sax; Dwane Smith and Don Gardner, tenor sax; Gary Hypes, baritone sax; Dave Stone, bass; Carlos Vega and Neal Finn, drums; Mike Higgins, guitar; Bob Bauer, piano; directed by Ladd McIntosh, with guest stars Mundell Lowe, Clark Terry, Ray Brown, Max Roach, Bill Watrous, Roy Burns. (The kids liked Bill Watrous the best. He talks out of the side of his mouth and plays beautifully.)

Sunday Evening, September 23, at 7:15 p.m.: "Family Night"
The Jones Boys: Thad and Elvin.
The Heath Boys: Percy, Tootie and Jimmy.
The Candoli Boys: Conte and Pete.
The Turrentine Boys: Stanley and Tommy.
Mr. and Mrs. Kral, Jackie and Roy.
Jimmy and Stacy Rowles.
The Thad Jones-Mel Lewis Big Band, Jon Faddis, Steve Furtado, Jim Bossy, Cecil Bridgewater, trumpets; Jimmy Knepper, Billy Campbell, Quentin Jackson, Cliff Heather, trombones; Jerry Dodgian, Eddie Xiques, Billy Harper, Ron Bridgewater, Pepper Adams, saxophones; Roland Hanna, piano; George Mraz, bass; Dee Dee Bridgewater, vocal.

* * *

If anything symbolized what Monterey had become, it was family night. The Festival had become a family of musicians, most of them from Los Angeles, most of them mainstream, most of them big banders. With the kids' concerts it was something like a fathers and sons atmosphere. It was wholesome jazz. Gone were the mysterious shaded childless, fatherless creatures who played into bent horns and smoked dope and shot up in toilets and mumbled in slang. Here were sunburnt musicians who owned houses, who had children and wives and cars, who were . . . well, who were American middle class mainstream U.S.A. And the kids were from the suburbs. This is where jazz was heading.

Program Cover, 1973

Max Roach with a few words to say about Jimmy Lyons, 1973

The Thad Jones-Mel Lewis Orchestra, 1973

Bobby Blue Bland, 1975

Dancing in the aisle to Bobby Blue Bland, 1975

1974

Duke Ellington, one of the Monterey family elders, passed away this year. The Festival was dedicated to Duke Ellington. He had written for the Festival, starred at the Festival, hosted the Festival, brought guests to the Festival. In the Monterey film, made almost ten years ago, Duke opens in a long moody shot along the ocean. If there is anything Jimmy Lyons has tried to live up to, it's been the style and grace of Mr. Ellington.

There was an unfortunate plane delay this year. It cost McCoy Tyner his Saturday night spot on the program. He came late and there was no time to squeeze him in at the end of the program. (Monterey evening concerts end at midnight.) So the already criticized Festival received more criticism for pushing around McCoy Tyner, a man who could be associated with the avant garde.

Friday Evening, September 20, at 9:00 p.m.:
Monterey Jazz Festival Quartet, with John Lewis, piano; Mundell Lowe, guitar; Richard Davis, bass; Roy Burns, drums; with Dizzy Gillespie, trumpet; Gerry Mulligan, baritone sax; Illinois Jacquet, tenor sax.
International Piano Forum, with Eubie Blake, George Shearing, Martial Solal, Dillwyn Jones, pianos; with Richard Davis, Mundell Lowe, Roy Burns.
Miss Sarah Vaughan.
Toshiyuki Miyama and the New Herd (from Japan), Toshiyuki Miyama, leader; Kazumi Takeda, Yoshikazu Kishi, Fumio Shirayama, Shigeru Kamimori, trumpets; Teruhiko Kataoka, Masamichi Uetaka, Takashi Hayakawa, Takahide Uchida, trombones; Koji Suzuki, Atsuo Shirai, alto saxes; Mamoru Mori, Seiji Inoue, tenor saxes; Kenichi Tada, baritone sax; Kiyoshi Takano, piano; Masaaki Ito, bass; Isao Yomoda, drums; Kozaburo Yanaki, guitar and arranger. (This was recorded: "The New Herd at Monterey," Trio Records, PA 3038-39M.)

Saturday Afternoon, September 21, at 1:30 p.m.:
Reverend Pearly Brown, guitars, mandolin, accordian, vocals; Christine Brown, vocals.

Sunnyland Slim and the Blue Spirit Band, Sunnyland Slim, piano and vocals; Harry Duncan, harmonica; Alan Hightman, guitar; Tom Patterson, bass; Levi Warren, drums.
James Cotton Blues Band, James Cotton, harmonica and vocals; Matt "Guitar" Murphy, guitar; Charles Camese, bass; Ken Johnson, drums; Little Bo, tenor sax.
Big Joe Turner.
Eddie "Cleanhead" Vinson.
Dizzy Gillespie.
Bo Diddley with Cookie Vee and the Peggy Malone Blues Band.
Jon Hendricks, host and Master of Ceremonies.

Saturday Evening, September 21, at 8:15 p.m.:
(McCoy Tyner was scheduled to open. His quartet—Azar Lawrence, Guillermi Franco, Joony Booth, Wilby Fletcher—was ready, but McCoy was late, so the house quartet went on.)
A Guitar Summit Session with Mundell Lowe, Joe Pass, Jim Hall, Michael Howell, Lee Ritenour, guitars; with John Lewis, Richard Davis, Roy Burns.
Miss Anita O'Day with the MJF quartet.
Dizzy Gillespie Quartet, Dizzy Gillespie, trumpet; Earl May, bass; Al Gafa, guitar; Mickey Roker, drums; special guests, Roy Eldridge, Clark Terry, Harry "Sweets" Edison.

Sunday Afternoon, September 22, at 12:30 p.m.:
Sunday afternoon (pre-concert) featured the combo and big band winners of the Fourth Annual California High School Jazz Band Competition. (No one was coming to the Sunday afternoon concerts, so Lyons moved up the regular concert an hour later, and put these groups on early.)
Grant Union High School, Sacramento, combo division winners: Leon Garner, piano; Randy Richards, bass; Esteban Rodriguez, drums; Mike Brookins, guitar; Jerome Thornton, conga; Joe Espinoza, alto sax; Ed Simental, tenor sax; Ike Paggett, director.
Eagle Rock High School, Los Angeles, jazz band division winners: Bob Musingo, Roger Ingram, Phillip Krumal, Harry Danser, Jim Stevenson, trumpets; Dave Rinaldo, Bob Haviland, Frank Marino, Dean Montgomery,

trombones; Doug Rinaldo, Lisa Moore, alto saxes; Patrick Ingram, Cindy Torres, tenor saxes; George Handy, baritone sax; Guy Steiner, Sandra Adams, Diana Clifford, pianos; Greg Calvillo, bass; Mike Freeman, guitar. John Rinaldo, director.

Regular concert:

Jazz Stars of Today and Tomorrow.

Chuck Mangione Quartet, Chuck Mangione, flugelhorn; Gerry Niewood, flute and saxophones; E. Williams, bass; Joe La Barbera, drums.

California All-Star High School Jazz Band: Mike Ernst, Roger Ingram, Kevin Bartlett, Kevin Mason, Ron Coolidge, trumpets; Doug Rinaldo, Leslie Nitta, Dwayne Smith, Marc Russo, Gary Hypes, saxophones; Steve Holtman, Bruce Holloway, Bill Snyder, Charles Morillas, John Zontek, trombones; Terry Lowe, piano; Lawrence Hart, bass; Carlos Vega, drums; Rick Jensen, percussion; Joe Movich, guitar; directed by Ladd McIntosh and Don Schamber, with guests, Dizzy Gillespie, Gerry Mulligan, Ladd McIntosh, William O. Smith, Clark Terry, Chuck Mangione.

Lowell High School of San Francisco concert orchestra, directed by Jack Pereira, with Amy Lozano, concertmaster; Robert Rinehart, assistant concertmaster; Dennis Bates, Steve Gold, Toi Jones, Kyoko Kishi, Mary Lazzareschi, Roxanne Michaelian, Mary Purcell, Anne Sachs, Seth Taylor, Maria Walsh, Dayna Yearwood, violins; Ah Ling Nev, Terry Carl, Louis Mannapau, Gina Scott, Tammy Cognetta, violas; Elizabeth Van Loon, Claire Li, Elizabeth Varnhagen, Gail Oliver, celli; Anita Piccone, bass viol; Phil Freihofner, Janet Popesco, oboes; Phil Freihofner, English horn; Karla Ekholm, Wendy Young, bassoons; Bill Hamaker, Tom Hernandez, Jane Pon, Lewis Lopez, French horn; Tony Blake, tympani; Courtenay Hardy, flute and piccolo; Frank Machia, clarinet.

Gerry Mulligan

Sunday Evening, September 22, at 7:15 p.m.:

Cal Tjader Quintet, Cal Tjader, vibes; Frank Strazzeri, piano; Harvey Newmark, bass; Dick Berk, drums; Michael Smithe, congas.

Jerome Richardson.

Mongo Santamaria.

Airto and "Fingers," Airto Moreira, percussion; Mike Wolff, piano; Barry Finnerty, guitar; Charles Fambro, bass; Roberto Silva, percussion.

"A Latin Jam—Inventions on Manteca," with Toshiyuki Miyama and the New Herd, and Dizzy Gillespie, Clark Terry, Cal Tjader, Jerome Richardson, Mongo Santamaria, and other guests.

Richard Leos, host and Master of Ceremonies.

A tribute to the Duke; left to right: Joe Pass, Jim Hall, Mundell Lowe, Michael Howell, Lee Ritenour, 1974

Airto Moreira, 1974

135

1975

Ralph Gleason, one of the inspirations of the Festival, died in June, 1975. The Festival started a memorial fund, $1,000 awarded yearly to a writer or critic in the field of jazz or other popular music.

It was Gleason who encouraged Lyons to find a place outdoors, to find a place away from the sultry, dark, webby settings of clubs; to put music out in the open. He and Lyons had spent many late, dank evenings in tiny clubs, listening to jazz and arguing which is better, pot or alcohol. As Jimmy tells it:

"I was sitting with Ralph in the Blackhawk one night and he pulled out a joint. He said, 'Why do you drink so much?'

"I said, 'Why do you smoke that?'

"He said, 'Listen, you stick to your shit and I'll stick to mine.'"

Gleason was a newspaper writer. He didn't let Lyons get away with a thing. A staunch defender of the early Festivals, he became a harsh critic of the latter ones. They were monotonous, conservative, familiar, he argued. Lyons would rave back at him. They were friends till the end.

Gleason would have found fault with this one too. But it had its moments.

The program opened with an old time jazz group, Barry Martyn and the Legends of Jazz. Barry Martyn, drums; Brother Cornbread, clarinet; Andrew Blakeney, trumpet; Alton Purnell, piano and vocal; Ed "Montudie" Garland, bass; Louis Nelson, trombone.

Friday Evening continued:

The Piano Playhouse, with John Lewis, Bill Evans, Marian McPartland, Patrice Rushen (a graduate of the high school competitions), and the MJF rhythm section, Mundell Lowe, Richard Davis and Roy Burns.

Helen Humes accompanied by Gerald F. Wiggins.

Toshiko Akiyoshi-Lew Tabackin Big Band, with Bobby Shew, Lynn Nicholson, Larry Ford, Mike Price, trumpets; Britt Woodman, Charlie Loper,

Jim Sawyer, Phil Teele, trombones; Andy MacIntosh, Gary Foster, Tom Peterson, Lew Tabackin, Bill Perkins, saxophones; Bob Daugherty, bass; Peter Donald, drums; Toshiko Akiyoshi, piano.

Saturday Afternoon, September 20, at 1:30 p.m.:

The Meters, with Joseph Modeliste, drums; Arthur Neville, keyboards; Leo Noccentelli, guitar; George Porter, Jr., bass; Cyril Neville, congas.

Sunnyland Slim, piano; Big Walter Horton, harmonica; Robert Lockwood, guitar; Skip Olson, bass; Francis Clay, drums; George "Harmonica" Smith, harmonica.

Etta James and friends.

Bobby "Blue" Bland with Melvin Jackson, Tommy Purkson, Joseph Harding, trumpets; Harold Potier, Charles Polk, drums; Louis Valeri, bass; Theodore Arthur, tenor saxophone; Al Thomas, trombone; Jim Karr, Mel Brown, guitars.

Saturday Evening, September 20, at 8:15 p.m.:

"Jazz Vignettes" with John Lewis, Paul Desmond, Benny Golson, "Toots" Thielmans, Clark Terry, Svend Asmussen, Richard Davis, Mundell Lowe, Roy Burns and Albert Mangelsdorff.

Helen Merrill and friends.

Chuck Mangione Quartet, Chuck Mangione, fluegelhorn; Gerry Niewood, flute and saxophones; Chip Jackson, bass; Joe La Barbera, drums.

Ed Shaughnessy Energy Force Big Band: John Audino, Stew Blumberg, Don Rader, Ron King, trumpets; Bob Payne, Jack Redmond, Bill Reichenbach, trombones; Lanny Morgan, Glen Garrett, Tom Peterson, Bob Cooper; John Mitchell, saxophones; Dave Parlota, bass; Peter Woodford, guitar; Greg Matheison, piano; David Levine, percussion; Ed Shaughnessy, acoustic and electric drums; Diane Schuur, vocalist.

Sunday Afternoon, September 21, at 12:30 p.m.:

Pre-concert, featuring combo and big band winners of the Fifth Annual California High School Jazz Band Competition.

Combo winner: Berkeley High School, Berkeley. Peter Apfelbaum, saxophone; Rodney Franklin, piano; Tony Williams, drums; Harold Foreman, bass; Phil Hardymon, director.

Band winner: Richmond High School, Richmond. Larry Lee, Larry Mah, Eric Wittig, Sheryl Shattuck, Clay Hanel, Dean Ito, saxophones; Ron Vallo, Keith Riley, Rod Citty, John Pitts, Adam Ellis, trombones; Scot Scofield, Bruce Spurlock, Jeff Eddings, Rod Jones, Sid Castillo, trumpets; Dion Duncan, Dave Hiatt, Sue Shinagawa, Jeff Glivas, Dale Nabeta, Mike Politeau, Preston Kauk, rhythm. Jay W. Lehmann, director.

Regular Concert:

California All-Star High School Jazz Band: Mike Breitsprecher, Roger Ingram, Brian Pearcy, Kevin Bartlett, Ron Coolidge, trumpets; Ted Nash, Eric Marienthal, Jack Irby, Loran McClung, Steve Bergman, saxophones; Paul Peterson, Joe Alessi, Chris Braymen, Luman Hughes, trombones; Donald Robinson, bass trombone; Randy Kerber, piano; Paul Magpusao, guitar; Greg Calvillo, bass; David Hocker, drums; Joe Caploe, vibes. Directed by Ladd McIntosh and Don Schamber; special guests, Benny Golson, John Lewis, Bill Evans, Pat Williams, Chuck Mangione.

Oakland Youth Symphony Orchestra: Jane Berger, Jeremy C. Cohen, Don Dimmitt, Daniel A. Fletcher, Anita Grunwald, Ruth Kahn, Mary Larionoff, Dan Pinkham, Sami Abdul-Rahim, Carlos A. Reyes, Sam Roth, Whitney Stephenson, Seth Taylor, Vivian Wolf, violins; Anne Lokken, Therese Carl, Renata Norcia, Greg Taboloff, violas; Brent Bove, Joel Cohen, Gloria Lum, Emil Miland, celli; Ida Bodin, Carla Lemon, basses; Rick Clark, tuba; Diane Koregelos, oboe; Karla Ekholm, Andy Radford, bassoons; Colleen Castle, Peter Douglas, John Gustely, Doug Kimball, French horns. Directed by Denis de Coteau.

Sunday Evening, September 21, at 7:15 p.m.:

Dizzy Gillespie Quartet, Dizzy Gillespie, trumpet; Earl May, bass; Al Gafa, guitar; Mickey Roker, drums; special guests, Cal Tjader, Kwaku Dadey and Luis O. Peralta, and others.

Betty Carter with the Alfred "Chip" Lyles Trio.

"Point of View," the Monterey Jazz Festival Quartet with Svend Asmussen, violin, and Hubert Laws, flute, in compositions by John Lewis.

Blood, Sweat and Tears: David Clayton-Thomas, vocals; Bobby Colomby, drums and background vocals; Dave Bargeron, trombones, tuba, trumpets, conga; Joe Giorgianni, trumpet, fluegelhorn, and piccolo; Tony Klatka, saxophone, trumpet, trombone; Ron McClure, electric and acoustic bass; Larry Willis, keyboards; Bill Tillman, saxophones, flutes, and background vocals.

*   *   *

The Festival had the inevitable L.A. big bands, Ed Shaughnessy and Akiyoshi-Tabackin, this year, but it also had lots of rock. The Meters and Bobby Bland and Blood, Sweat and Tears, and Chuck Mangione, who was bringing jazz closer to rock. (Blood, Sweat and Tears was bringing rock closer to jazz.)

Ed Shaughnessy brought with him a tremendous singer named Diane Schuur who sang like Aretha Franklin. She's somewhere in L.A. today, disappearing in the huge music world.

Paul Desmond, 1975

Betty Carter, 1975

Marian McPartland, left, and Patrice Rushen, 1975

1976

The Bicentennial Festival. Big band retrospectives and recreations of old band music: Jimmie Lunceford and Fletcher Henderson. The Festival of tributes: to bop, to Louis, to Duke. Count Basie was scheduled to recreate his Kansas City Seven, but Basie had a heart attack and couldn't make it. He'd come back in '77, his band cooking as hard as ever.

But it took a 9-piece college band from the Midwest—Matrix—to get the audience on its feet. It was the first standing ovation at Monterey in five years and it happened because the band had energy, youth, and nobody'd ever heard of them. Which meant there was a surprise. Something Monterey had too little of in recent years.

The show opened with the Olympia Brass Band from New Orleans, the great funeral band. They were so happy to be playing, they started every concert half an hour early. You can't stop them.

The Olympia Brass Band: Harold Dejan, Emanuel Paul, saxophones; Anthony Lacen, tuba; Andrew Jefferson, snare drum; Nowell Glass, bass drum; Gerald Joseph, Frank Naundorf, trombones; George Colar, trumpet; Edmond Foucher, Milton Batiste, fluegelhorns and trumpets; Anderson Stewart, Grand Marshall; Richard Matthew, percussion.

Then came the big band retrospectives:

The music of Fletcher Henderson with the Bill Berry Monterey Jazz Festival All-Star Band, featuring Russell Procope; directed by Benny Carter. Bill Berry, Gene Goe, Cat Anderson, Blue Mitchell, Jack Sheldon, trumpets; Jimmy Cleveland, Britt Woodman, Tricky Lofton, Benny Powell, trombones; Marshall Royal, Don Menza, Richie Kamuca, Lanny Morgan, Jack Nimitz, saxophones; Frank Capp, drums; Monte Budwig, bass; Dave Frischberg, piano.

A Tribute to Louis Armstrong, featuring Doc Cheatham, Harry "Sweets" Edison, Dizzy Gillespie, Clark Terry, and Benny Carter with the Monterey Jazz Festival Quartet, John Lewis, Mundell Lowe, Roy Burns, Richard Davis.

The Music of Jimmy Lunceford with the Festival All-Star Band under the direction of Gerald Wilson, and featuring Snooky Young.

A Tribute to BeBop, with the Dizzy Gillespie Quartet, with Rodney Jones, guitar; Benjamin Franklin Brown, bass; Mickey Roker, drums; and guests Benny Golson and Sonny Criss.

Saturday Afternoon, September 18, at 12:30 p.m.:

Pre-concert: the combo and big band winners of the California high school competitions.

Berkeley High School, Berkeley, combo winners: Peter Apfelbaum, saxophone; Rodney Franklin, piano; Tony Williams, drums; Harold Foreman, bass; Phil Hardymon, director.

Reseda High School, Reseda, jazz band winners: Mike Delwarte, John Wolfe, Jim Rogers, Don Stillo, Rubbie Goldfield, trumpets; Grant Keary, Brian Mathison, Mark Urwiller, Mark Ludiner, Rick Austinson, trombones; Sara Lokkeu, French horn; Kris Klavik, DeEuva Urwiller, Ted Nash, Chris Allen, Danny Robin, saxophones; Randy Kerber, piano; Stacey de Hart, bass; Scott Klein and Jay Setar, drums; John Patka, guitar; Len Gagliardi, director.

Regular Concert:

The Olympia Brass Band.

A Gospel Invocation with the Seaside Bethel Baptist Church Choir.

Queen Ida and the Bon Ton Zydeco Band.

Country Blues with Joe "Willie" Wilkins, Johnny Shines, and the Hollywood Fats Blues Band.

Urban Blues with Margie Evans, Jimmy Witherspoon, James Cotton and his Chicago Blues Band.

Saturday Evening, September 18, at 8:15 p.m.:
The Olympia Brass Band.

Commemorating the Duke with the Festival Orchestra featuring Russell Procope, Cat Anderson, Clark Terry and Gerald Wilson, under the direction of Bill Berry.

Miss Helen Humes, and Gerald Wiggins, accompanist.

The Paul Desmond Quartet, featuring Ed Bickert, guitar; Don Thompson, bass; Jerry Fuller, drums.

Paul Desmond

The Music of Count Basie—a Basie Retrospective by the Kansas City Seven (with Nat Pierce sitting in for the ailing Basie), with Vic Dickenson, Harry "Sweets" Edison, Buddy Tate, and others. The Count Basie Band with vocalist Helen Humes. Freddie Green, guitar; Charles "Butch" Miles, drums; John Heard, bass; George "Sonny" Cohn, George "Pete" Minger, Robert Mitchell, Lyn Biviano, trumpets; Robert Plater, Eric Dixon, Jimmy Forrest, Charlie Fowlkes, saxophones; Danny Turner, William Hughes, Melvin Wanzo, Curtis Fuller, Albert Grey, trombones; Bill Caffie, vocals.

Sunday Afternoon, September 19, at 1:30 p.m.:
The Olympia Brass Band.
The All-California High School Jazz Band, directed by Ladd McIntosh and Don Schamber, performing new works by McIntosh, Schamber

and Jimmy Heath. Mike Plumleigh, Mike Breitsprecher, Jim Dunn, Steve Mortenson, Chad Wackerman, trumpets; Ted Nash, Eric Marienthal, Carl Jones, David Camp, Jeff Grubic, saxophones; Chris Braymen, Joseph Alessi, Jeff Enloe, Steve Montenson, Donald Robinson, trombones; Randy Kerber, piano; Larry Koonse, guitar; Brice Wightman, bass; Chad Wackerman, Mike Guerra, percussion. (They come from all over the state: Huntington Beach, Mira Loma, Palm Springs, Pleasant Hill, Corona Del Mar, Monterey, Berkeley, Terra Linda, Sacramento. They come eager and they come ready to play.)

The Heath Brothers Quartet, Percy Heath, bass; James Heath, saxophone; Albert Heath, drums; Stanley Cowell, piano.

Afro-American Suite of Evolution: African Percussion—Crossing—Field Holler—Spiritual—Street Band—Ragtime—Blues—Boogie Woogie—Swing—BeBop—Samba-Ballad—R & B—Avant Garde. With Kwaku Dadey, drums; Joe Turner, vocals; the Festival All-Star Band; the Bethel Baptist Church Singers; the Oakland Youth Symphony Strings: James Berger, Fay Chan, Dan Dimmitt, Brad Irving, Peter Kupfer, Whitney Stephenson, Karen Thurman, Dan Tinkham, violins; Debbie Dare, Marsha Gonick, Renata Norcia, Jennifer Sills, violas; Jimmy Culp, Emil Miland, celli. Directed by Jimmy Heath, the composer.

Sunday Evening, September 19, at 7:30 p.m.:
The Olympia Brass Band.
Matrix: directed by John Harmon; Fred Sturm, trombone; John Harmon, keyboards; Mike Hale, trumpet; Randall Fird, bass; Kurt Deitrich, trombone; Larry Darling, trumpet; Michael Bard, saxophone; Gary Miller, drums; Jeff Pietrangelo, trumpet.

Eje Thelin Quartet, New Directions in Swedish Jazz.

The Cal Tjader Quintet, Cal Tjader, vibes; Peter Riso, drums; Rob Fisher, bass; Frank Mercurio, piano; Pancho Sanchez, conga drums; and the Latin Infusion, with guests Carmelo Garcia, Rob Redfield and Luis Gasca.

The Toshiko Akiyoshi-Lew Tabackin Big Band—A summation: Jazz, An International Art Form.

Jimmy Heath conducts the "Afro-American Suite of Evolution," 1976

Lew Tabackin and Toshiko Akiyoshi, 1975

Toshiko Akiyoshi and the Lew Tabackin Band, 1975

1977

What started as a little affair to bring jazz out in the open made it through 20 years. It made it and will continue making it because it's Jimmy Lyons' life. He lives for that damn Festival. No matter how hard the critics knock it. Jimmy Lyons lives day in and day out for those three days, that third weekend in September. His best friends are people he might see just those three days a year. John Lewis or Dizzy Gillespie or Cal Tjader or Mundell Lowe. He's sort of like a hermit crab who lives in this tiny rock, talking on the phone, and then he comes off that rock, flies down to Monterey and has three swell days, boy. Nervous days, tense days, you can't talk to him. But, Jesus Christ, he lives to see those high school kids come down there and blow everyone off the stage. He lives to hear them noodling in their hotel rooms. He lives to hear their excitement. He lives to hear and see an unannounced guest come strolling across the stage in the middle of someone's set and start jamming. Clark Terry or Dizzy or Mulligan.

He stands backstage peering out, chewing his damn thumbs, this quiet, fatherly crab, staring out at these black and white and yellow faces. Always sold out now. Each concert jammed. And he can be proud of that. He can be proud of how little violence has occurred through the years. He can be proud that the Festival now is totally integrated, when, in the beginning, so long ago, people were reticent about renting rooms to black people.

There wasn't any trouble. The black people came, the white people came, the Japanese came from Japan, the Europeans from Europe, for those three days.

It's like a wild, comical party out there in the audience. They drink, they smoke, they poke shoulders, they lust around, they listen when they feel like it, they bundle up, they strip down, they dance, they rock, they curse, they like the big bands, they hate the big bands, they tune in and they tune out.

There aren't as many high points any more. One or two a Festival. Mostly it's big band music, blues and ballads you've heard before. But there's always a moment or two, a surprise, an unexpected chilling solo, and you always leave with something to talk about.

1977 was the year when the high school kids knocked everyone out. They just played with so much guts and energy and spirit. What used to be the part of the Festival everyone would sleep through became a part of the Festival you wouldn't want to miss. That energy, the energy that's usually associated with far out, creative elements of jazz, is what the kids have. That desire to push the music as far as it will go.

The hits of this Festival were clearly the kids and Butch Miles (Count Basie's drummer—he never stopped smiling when he played; it wasn't a phony smile) and Ted Curson who had played the Festival in the early years (1962). Ted Curson looked out of place. He said he felt like the token avant gardist.

Festivals all over Europe, especially Nice, were so much grander than Monterey, featuring so many different kinds of jazz.

But Monterey is a small festival. It's not a money making festival. Its profits go to support young musicians. So in a way it's unfair to compare it to George Wein's circuses. Monterey's an intimate, family gathering. More Europeans are coming, more Japanese are coming. At one point during this Festival Jimmy Lyons was being interviewed by nearly a dozen radio programs. Almost all of them would be broadcast overseas.

Jazz has never been more popular, and in a way Jimmy Lyons is responsible for some of that popularity. He's sponsored the next generation of jazz. The kids. He's sponsored the acceptance of jazz in schools. Jazz musicians aren't going to be junkies anymore, not so easily anyway; they're not going to be on the fringes of the underworld. They're right in there next to the lawyers and salesmen and businessmen and teachers.

There might have been one Los Angeles big band too many at Monterey, but there'll never be enough gorgeous kids lugging their instruments to the rehearsals, taking jazz into the next decade.

This year's Festival:

Friday Evening, September 16, at 9:00 p.m.:
The Airmen of Note (U.S. Air Force Jazz Band) playing the premiere of a specially-commissioned work, "The Happy Birthday Monterey Suite," composed and conducted by Gerald Wilson; special guests, Clark Terry, Mundell Lowe, Eddie "Lockjaw" Davis. The Airmen: John Dodge, Gene Gaydos, Roger Hogan, Les Whittington, reeds; Ken Smukal, Jim Lay, Larry Trautman, Bruce Nelson, trumpets; Dave Steinmeyer, Gary Hall, Rick Lillard, Mark Madden, trombones; Gil Cray, piano; Rick Whitehead, guitar; Brent McKesson, bass; Frank Shaffer, drums; directed by Ernest Hensley.

The Ted Curson Quartet featuring David Friesen, with Ted Curson, trumpet; David Friesen, bass; Ronnie Steen, drums; Nick Brignola, saxophone; Jim McNeely, piano.

Joe Williams, accompanied by the MJF Quartet: John Lewis, Mundell Lowe, Richard Davis, Roy Burns.

Count Basie and his Orchestra (Basie back, healthy, sparse and beaming).

Saturday Afternoon, September 17, at 1:30 p.m. (this concert was sold out months in advance):
Mardi Gras at Monterey:
Queen Ida and her Bon Ton Zydeco Band.
Professor Longhair, with the Neville Brothers rhythm section: Rodger Poche, bass; Renard Poche, guitar; Newton Mossap, drums.
Clarence "Gatemouth" Brown, with Gregg Mazell, reeds; Eugene Ross, guitar; David Keller, bass; Ben Culley, drums.

The Neville Brothers, Art, Aaron, Cyril and Charles, with Gerald Tillman, keyboards; Rodger Poche, bass; Renard Poche, guitar; Newton Mossap, drums.
The Wild Tchoupitoulas (the Nevilles) with Big Chief Jolly (uncle to the Nevilles).

Saturday Evening, September 17, at 8:15 p.m.:
The Airmen of Note, in a new work by John Lewis, with Mr. Lewis at the piano.
Piano Summit with John Lewis and Hank Jones in a duet.
Carrie Smith and the MJF Quartet.
The Horace Silver Quintet, with Thomas Harrell, trumpet; Lawrence Schneider, saxophone; Chip Jackson, bass; and Edward Gladden, drums.
"20th Anniversary Blowout," a giant jam session with Clark Terry, Harry "Sweets" Edison, Eddie "Lockjaw" Davis, Benny Golson, John Lewis, Richard Davis, Mundell Lowe, Roy Burns, Gary Foster, Cal Tjader, and other guests (among them Go Yamamoto, a young Japanese piano player, who walked on unannounced, played a tune, and stole the jam).

Sunday Afternoon, September 18, at 1:30 p.m.:
The California High School All-Star Jazz Band: Mike Plumleigh, Buddy Gordon, Herbert Sneed, Jenny Stoik, Mike Delwarte, trumpets; Ted Nash (his third Festival—he was on leave from the Don Ellis Big Band), Dan Wilensky, Dalton Hagler, Ray Clement, Keith Squyres, reeds; Steve Mortensen, Scott Kyle, Phillip Agretelis, Mario Sternad, Duane Grubert, trombones; Larry Koonse, guitar; Bill Beaver, bass; Murray Low, piano; Cary Avery, percussion; Scott Klein, drums. Directed by Benny Golson and Don Schamber, featuring new works by Benny Golson, Dan Schamber, Clark Terry, and Alan Yankee, who had played here with the first high school band eight years ago.

The Contemporary Keyboard Suite by George Duke, featuring Mr. Duke and the High School All-Star Jazz Band in a work commissioned by *Contemporary Keyboard Magazine*.

Percussion Profiles with George Gruntz, featuring Jack DeJohnette, Dom Um Romao, Pierre Favre and Fredy Studer, percussion; David Friedman, vibes; commissioned by Paiste Cymbals.

Sunday Evening, September 18, at 7:30 p.m.:

Matrix: Mike Hale, Michael Bard, Jeff Pietrangelo, Larry Darling, Kurt Dietrich, Fred Sturm, John Harmon, Randall Fird and Gary Miller, all on multiple instruments.

The Aldeberts, with Billy Childs, keyboard; Larry Klein, bass; Dave Igelfeld, drums.

Art Blakey and the Jazz Messengers, with Walter Davis, piano; Valeri Pononarev, trumpet; Robert Watson, David Schnitter, saxophones; Dennis Irwin, bass. (Art Blakey plays with a big open smile too. It's the kind of smile people wear when things come easy and natural to them. Most jazz musicians look mean when they play. It's probably because jazz is so hard to play and takes so long to learn, it makes you mad and frustrated. It's also tough to smile when you're concentrating so hard. Then there's the kind of playing that's almost found; and you say, smiling, "Look, look what I can do." That's what Art Blakey is saying.)

Betty Carter with John Hicks, piano; Calvin Hill, bass; Cliff Barbera, drums.

Tito Puente and his Orchestra, with Martin Oberlanson, Albert Shikaly, Julio Rodriquez, Manuel Santos, Paulo de Paula, David Tucker, Vincent Frisaura, Francisco Pastor, Nilo Sierra, Michael Colloro, Jose Madera, Luis Bouza, Frank Figueroa, Rafael Barbosa and Richard Pullin. Special guest, Cal Tjader.

* * *

The Festival ended, 7,000 people dancing to Puente in the rain.

Happy Anniversary—20 years of jazz at Monterey, 1977

Art Blakey, 1977

Ted Curson, 1977

Tito Puente and his orchestra, 1977

Horace Silver, 1977

Singer Carrie Smith with, left to right: Mundell Lowe, Roy Burns, Clark Terry, 1977

Conducting, Count Basie style, 1977

Butch Miles on drums, 1977

The 1977 California All-Star High School Jazz Band

Monterey jam; left to right: John Lewis, Richard Davis, Clark Terry, Mundell Lowe, Harry Edison, Roy Burns (on drums), Benny Golson, Eiji Kitamura, Cal Tjader, Eddie "Lockjaw" Davis, 1977

Gleanings: Highlights, Sidelights, & Opinions Pro and Con

Following are just a few of the thousands of articles about jazz and the Monterey Jazz Festival that have been published in the past twenty years in the media and in the Festival's own annual programs.

David Stone Martin

Argot of Jazz–1958

by Elliot Horne

One of the most striking side effects of jazz, an American invention, is the language around it. When jazz changes, the slang changes. What was "hep" nearly two decades ago will not be "hip" today. The phenomenal growth of modern jazz in the last few years has given rise to a good many new terms, some specimens of which follow:

ALWAYS IN THE CELLAR–A horn man who always blows in a low register.

AX–Any musical instrument, even a piano.

BEAR–An unattractive girl.

BEARD–An avant garde type; also a hipster.

BELLS–Vibraphones.

BLOW–To play a musical instrument, any instrument. Thus, "He blows fine piano." Also to perform any act: "He blows great conversation," "She blows scrambled eggs from endville." Endville (obs.) means the best.

BLOWS FOR CANINES–Plays long successions of high notes; screeches.

BOGUE–Fake, phony, false, bogus.

BOX–Piano.

BREAD–Money. See also Geets, Green and "M."

BUSTER–Generic for a guy with no future and not much of a past, either.

CHARTS–Musical arrangements. See also Maps.

COMMERCIAL–Request numbers. Usually played by dance bands. Some hot bands pointedly ignore requests and will play a blues, for example, if asked for *Rosetta*.

CRUMBS–A small sum of money; also called small bread.

CUTTING A TAKE–Explaining a point. In the recording business, literally to make a record.

EYES TO COOL IT–The desire to relax, to get away from it all. To have eyes for anything is to want something, thus, "I got eyes to dig some sack time," meaning, "I'd like to get some sleep."

FAR OUT–Extremely advanced; gone; they don't run trains there any more. In music, modern jazz.

FINGER POPPER–A cat (musician or hipster) who is swinging.

GEETS–Money.

GO-IT-ALL–An automobile. See also Rubber, Short, and Wheels.

GREASE–To eat.

HANGIN'–Waiting around; sweating out a decision.

HAVE YOU SEEN MY HAT?–Have you seen my girl, chick, broad, rib?

HE SURE DID SPEAK–He played well or he blew great.

HE'S CLOSE MAN–The musician has done just about everything attainable on his ax, the cat digging him has been reached, i.e., the guy blowing has hit a nerve.

HEAVY CREAM–A fat girl.

HIDES–Drums.

HIPPY–Generic for a character who is supercool, overblase, so far out that he appears to be asleep when he's digging something the most.

I'M SORRY, MAN–Expression of disagreement; bewilderment; failure to reach any conclusion.

J. C.–James Caesar Petrillo, former president of the American Federation of Musicians.

LEFNA–Generic for Buster's wife, who is always deriding him for being nowhere.

LIVING ROOM GIG–A guest appearance in television. A gig is middle-musicianese for any job.

LOOSE WIG–A completely uninhibited, really way-out musician.

LYING–Playing the notes as written, rather than improvising on a theme; dogging it; playing with a sweet band rather than a hot one.

MAPS–Musical arrangements.

MEAN–The best; the greatest. See also Terrible and Tough.

MEET–A jam session. Thus, "Fall in, man, we're gonna make a meet in the p.m."

"M"–Money.

MONKEY–A music critic. (He sees no music, hears no music, digs no music.)

OOFUS–A dope; the kind of person who shows up at Monterey with a ticket for the Opera House.

OUT SACK–An attractive dress, a knockout.

PIPE–A saxophone.

PLEADING A FIVE–When one cat refuses to get up on the stand and blow with another. Derived from pleading the Fifth Amendment or refusing to talk.

SCENE–Any place where musicians play or gather; by extension, any place persons meet or any event they attend. Thus, "Let's make the country scene this weekend."

SECURITY CATS–Television or radio musicians under contract who work regularly, preferring the security of a weekly salary to gigging around with a band on different jobs.

SHE'S NUTS–The girl is a doll.

SHORT–An automobile.

SHUCKING–Bluffing, faking, vamping, playing chords when a cat doesn't know the melody.

SIS–A girl.

SKY–A hat.

SMALL PIPE–Alto saxophone. Also, Big Pipe or baritone saxophone.

SPLOUD!–High-spirited; happy; wild.

SOMETHING ELSE–A phenomenon so special it defies description. Thus, when asked if the music was great (or a gas), a cat may reply, "No, man, not that; it was something else."

STIFFIN' 'N' JIVIN'–Showing off or blowing high with lots of sound effect but not much musicianship.

TASTE–Usually a drink or some money. Can mean a portion of anything good.

TERRIBLE–The best; the greatest.

THE EARS ARE MOVING–An audience that is responsive.

THE MAN–The leader of a band.

THE NOOSE IS HANGING–All the musicians are primed for a cutting session, i.e., each man will attempt to outdo or cut the others.

THE SNAKE–The subway.

THERE'S NO MORE ROOM–An individual or group (musicians or otherwise) that are too much.

THEY REALLY WALK–The rhythm section really swings.

TOUGH–The best; the greatest.

TWISTED–Confused, mixed up, way too far out.

VEIN–The double bass.

VINES–Clothes. Formerly threads.

WAIL–To play, blow, or perform outstandingly. By extension, to do anything very well.

WANTS THE MOON–A cat who takes a melody for a wild ride, trying to do things his horn won't or can't.

WHEELS–Automobile.

WHIFFER–A flute.

WHO'S TAKIN' CARE OF BUSINESS?–Who's on the stand tonight?

YOU GET IT ALL–The answer to "What's new?" when a cat means "Nothing, man."

* * *

All those words seem so hokey and remote now. People who play jazz today talk like anyone else. They're no longer treated as freaks. Most of them learn jazz in schools and universities and practice in their parents' living rooms. The whole image of the mysterious hipster has puffed itself out.

Reprinted from Monterey Jazz Festival Program, 1958

Memories of Monterey
by Ralph J. Gleason

'59's Best Jazz Festival

The jazz festivals, which have become such a part of the summer season in this country, have tended to be musical circuses and as such have drawn to themselves much adverse comment from musicians.

The Monterey Jazz Festival, last month, was a shining exception. When it was over, the musicians unanimously agreed that it was the best festival of the year, the only one at which they felt completely at home.

"It was only the best jazz festival ever held," said John Lewis of the Modern Jazz Quartet. Gunther Schuller, who conducted part of the afternoon programs, agreed.

Several things marked Monterey as unique.

No one told the musicians what to play or what not to play. They were given full scope and plenty of time in which to state their piece.

The atmosphere was informal, rustic and utterly delightful in the pleasant California town. The citizens welcomed the musicians and the jazz fans.

No one used his appearance to plug his latest records.

The two afternoon programs were devoted to experimental modern music, almost all of it jazz. A rehearsal orchestra consisting of some of the most accomplished jazz musicians in the country (men like Ray Linn, Zoot Sims, Mel Lewis, Si Zentner, Conte Candoli, Med Flory, Bill Perkins, Richie Kamuca and Urbie Green) rehearsed for four days under the leadership of Woody Herman.

They played as the Herman band on one night, but in the afternoon programs they were the workshop orchestra for compositions by Benny Golson, Ernie Wilkins, John Lewis, Jay Jay Johnson and others. On one of the afternoons, augmented by members of the San Francisco Symphony, they performed some exciting modern music by Schuller ("Symphony for Brass and Percussion"), Lewis and Johnson.

"This was the greatest experience of my life," Mr. Johnson said afterwards and that comment was echoed again and again by musicians of all ranks.

Non-commerciality was the key note. This festival orchestra represented the first full scale attempt by a festival to allow jazz musicians freedom to experiment. John Lewis of the Modern Jazz Quartet was musical consultant to the festival and the afternoon programming was entirely in his hands.

Numerous musical moments provided great excitement for the well behaved and interested crowds that attended. Ben Webster, Jimmy Witherspoon, Lambert-Hendricks-Ross, Jay Jay Johnson, Zoot Sims and Earl Hines will be long remembered for the way they performed that week-end. But it was as a jazz festival in which the musicians themselves have a voice and an interest that Monterey has made its mark.

Monterey is really something different. The profits go to scholarships to the Monterey Peninsula College music department and the whole thing is a non-profit corporation sponsored by citizens of the city—lawyers, doctors, a meat dealer, a school controller, a printer, a newspaper editor, etc.

It is public service in a very real sense.

A Great Jazz Festival – 1960

Memories of Monterey—Helen Humes' electrifying opening chorus on "Please Don't Talk About Me When I'm Gone."

The conversation on the history of modern music between Gunther Schuller and Monterey Police Chief Charlie Simpson on the lawn Sunday morning.

The lack of attention paid to "Sheba, the Cat with Six Legs" on display in a trailer on the mall.

Musicians, customers and fans mixing in front of the art exhibit and Ornette Coleman, who judged it, picking Jules Erbit's "The Blues" with the comment, "It has the line and it swings." Erbit is a Hungarian who recently moved to Carmel.

Harry Carney peeking around the curtain on the stage to watch Jon Hendricks do his imitation of the bass players Saturday night.

The look on Odetta's face when The Andrews Sisters, the gospel quartet, sang on Sunday afternoon.

Ralph Gleason articles, pages 156-171, reprinted through the courtesy of the San Francisco Chronicle.

Gerry Mulligan's hairdo.

The Ellington band's looks of pleasure when Jimmy Rushing stomped on-stage Saturday night.

Ornette Coleman announcing "I was told to give the titles of the four tunes we will play, but they don't have any titles yet."

John Lewis stepping in at the last minute to play piano for Helen Humes because her accompanist, Gerald Wiggins, was grounded at Santa Barbara in a plane.

The free coffee at the Jazz Workshop's coffee bar.

The policeman who entered the rehearsal hall, stopped to listen to the music and, when told "You must be a real jazz fan," drawled, "No. I'm just the fuzz!"

The tears streaming down the faces of the audience and musicians at Jon Hendrick's "Evolution of the Blues Song" Sunday afternoon.

Annie Ross' fascinating changes of costume.

The fog swirling on-stage just when Jay Jay Johnson announced the title of his next number —"Minor Mist."

The bongo-playing collection of fans in one of the stalls on the exhibit line who dispersed after the Monterey police detachment squatted down alongside them. "We just sat down and communicated with them" Chief Simpson said.

Dave Topelis, who hitchhiked from Arizona for the third year to volunteer as a backstage helper.

The exciting combination of Jimmy Witherspoon's singing and the American Youth Band's playing Saturday afternoon on the mall.

Hannah Dean's prayer during Sunday's afternoon program.

Miriam Makeba.

Musicians shaking their heads and smiling during the "Evolution of the Blues Song" program.

Jay Jay Johnson's comment on Jon Hendricks' story that afternoon: "They're hearing the truth now!"

The performance of the Modern Jazz Quartet.

Zoot Sims' solos with the Gerry Mulligan band.

Odetta's unaccompanied singing of a work song.

Duke Ellington's explanation of the ritual of finger snapping and earlobe tilting.

The photographer from the Chinese edition of *Down Beat*.

© Jim Marshall

Miriam Makeba in "Evolution of the Blues Song," 1960

Big Miller and Jimmy Witherspoon.
Lambert-Hendricks-Ross singing "Cottontail."
Jon Hendricks' imitation of the bass players.
The crowds at the afternoon shows.
The feeling of warmth and of excitement that pervaded the entire musician cadre throughout the festival, with but very few exceptions.
The beautiful weather.

'Poor Butterfly,' Dizzy's Robe – 1961

The memories of the recent Monterey Jazz Festival: the breath condensing into wispy fog and floating out of the bell of Al Porcino's trumpet at midnight Friday when he played Louis Armstrong's "Jubilee" chorus . . . the harp player looking for a baby-sitter so she could attend a rehearsal . . . the signs up the road for fallout shelters.

The socialites laying cheek-by-jowl, so to speak, on the lawn with the Big Sur and North Beach Brigade . . . Max Weiss' astrakhan hat . *. Dizzy Gillespie's Yugoslavian shoes with the turned up tips . . . Duke Ellington's solo on "A Single Petal of a Rose" . . . Joe Carroll's great line, "Davy Crockett take your hand out of my pocket" . . . Johnny Hodges smiling when he was on stage with Jimmy Rushing . . .

. . . Stuff Smith and Ray Nance's duet on violin opening night . . . Lawrence Brown's solo on "Poor Butterfly" which remained, throughout the weekend, a subject of conversation among the audience . . . Paul Gonsalves' leap into the air and his kick before he began his solo Sunday night . . .

The dancers on the lawn . . . Dizzy's dedication of a number to the wife of the Chief of Police, Charles Simpson . . . Ernst's fans waving in the hot Sunday afternoon air . . . the lone man in the derby and chesterfield who walked across the arena Saturday night with a tray full of drinks . . . the absence of disc jockeys from the stage . . . Sam "Knuckles" Woodyard's solo without sticks or brushes . . . Chuck Lambkin's solo Sunday afternoon on "Gillespiana," in fact ALL of "Gillespiana" . . .

. . . The French horn players at the rehearsal when Dizzy sang them their parts . . . the look of awe on the trumpet sections' faces when, at rehearsal, Dizzy blew a few extra cadenzas . . . Jimmy Rushing singing "There'll Be Some Changes Made" in the rehearsal hall, with Ralph Sutton almost exploding with excitement and Stuffy Smith wailing away on the fiddle . . .

. . . Ben Webster taking pictures all weekend and especially the moment when he snapped the Terry Gibbs sax section while they were playing Ben's own solo from "Cottontail" which they had scored for five saxes . . . Dizzy playing for some kids by the back gate . . . the solitary tuba player at 10 p.m. Thursday night going through his part alone . . . the lady who wanted to reserve tickets now for next year.

Jimmy Lyons and Don Jeffries standing at the back of the arena, unrecognized, listening to the sound . . . the sound technicians at 4 a.m. putting the finishing touches on backstage . . . the Peacemobile parked outside the grounds . . . Chief of Police Charlie Simpson perched in his lookout post above the stands listening to Dizzy Gillespie and Joe Carroll . . .

. . . Virgil Gonsalves' party . . . Dizzy Gillespie answering the idiot at the press conference who was in love with the sound of his own voice . . . Gunther Schuller, J.J. Johnson and Dizzy congratulating one another backstage Sunday evening . . . J. J. Johnson's remark: "I decided not to worry about the brass section. Look at all those giants! I decided to worry about ME" . . .

The photographers clustered at Duke Ellington's feet when he was working as emcee from the small stage. . . . Duke's delight in playing his own favorite of his own compositions, "One More Time" . . . Dizzy saying he was combining the Nigerian robe and the Yugoslavian shoes in his own personal attempt to amalgamate the Balkans and Africa . . . Dizzy's announcement that he had changed the title of "A Night in Tunisia" to "A Night Away from Bizerte" because we wouldn't vote against France in the U.N.

Carmen McRae's visual and vocal beauty as she hushed 7,300 people Saturday with "When Sunny Gets Blue" . . . Duke Ellington's backstage dressing room decorated with flowers and a sign reading "Duke's Place" . . . Dizzy helping Gunther Schuller conduct . . . Lalo Schifrin's piano solo . . . the CRAZY weather and, of course, the girls in their summer dresses.

The 1962 Jazz Festival

Earl Hines, Rex Stewart and Al Porcino turning out to be vocalists. Mel Lewis and Buddy Clark, the work horses of the festival. The excitement of "The New Continent" both in the rehearsals and the final performance, especially the groove the band got into in the fourth and fifth movements. The nine saxophones massed on stage Saturday afternoon. Paul Desmond soloing in turn. Phil Woods' inspired alto solo on "The Midnight Sun Will Never Set," Quincy Jones' gorgeous composition. Al Porcino and his speeches. Bola Sete and Dizzy Gillespie exchanging dance steps and playing the tambourine Sunday afternoon. Dizzy taking pictures from underneath the stage, sticking his checkered hat up and blowing a cloud of smoke when Porcino's band played "Minor Walk."

Cartoonist Bill Bate's struggle to get his picture to come out on the clouded, mist-heavy screen—Kathy Jones getting tossed into the Mark Thomas pool Sunday afternoon.

Jeanne Lee and Ran Blake struggling helplessly against the noise backstage Sunday night. The wild uniforms of the band Saturday afternoon—from formal to tennis shoes and sweatsocks. The native uprising in the stable area with Congo drums and chanting all night long each night.

The kids perched on the roofs of the houses adjacent to the arena for the shows. The Dizzy Gillespie sweatshirts draped on the front boxes, worn by the crowds and posed in by the musicians in Dizzy's rehearsal. The KRON crew leaping with excitement. Saturday afternoon's weather switch.
Conte Candoli's look of pure admiration when Dizzy soloed. The guy with the Roman warrior sandals, the leather coming halfway up his leg. The other guy in Bermuda shorts in Saturday night's cold fog. The band congratulating each other in the Hunt Room after the Quincy Jones set Saturday.

Vince Guaraldi peering through the camera slot in the wing, his dark glasses and mustachios standing out against the pale color of the flat. Lalo Schifrin's smile when Bola Sete played. Tom Chestnut's French horn solo with Quincy Jones' band. Dizzy Gillespie wearing a purple ribbon from the Monterey County Fair, "Champion:

Hog Division," it said. Bill Harris shaking his head and saying "to get to play with guys like that," meaning Hines, Webster, and Stuff Smith, Rex Stewart and Co. The Casa Munras sign, "Weather today: Attuned."

Ben Webster first, then Jimmy Rushing, playing the piano at the rehearsal for the swing set Friday. "I hear you, Jimmy," Rex Stewart called out when Rushing sang. "How we gonna get out of this?" Benny Carter asked midway through the first tune at the rehearsal. The archers' bows and the bales of straw that are the targets for the archery club that meets in the rehearsal hall during regular time. They made a nice backdrop to the music. Larry Bunker's Aston-Martin. The marks on the Dizzy Gillespie French horn parts where previous players had signed their names. Dizzy Gillespie playing the conga drum in an hour-long jam session Friday afternoon. "I hope my hands don't swell," he said. The drums echoing on the empty grounds at midnight during the rehearsal evenings. Saxophonist Harold Wiley looking tanned and seaworthy after sailing down from San Francisco for the festival. "It took 28 hours," he said.

The photographers who were everywhere. The Benny Goodman stickers on Mel Lewis' drum kit, reminders of the Russian tour. "Buttermilk"—the gray horse owned by the daughter of the Fairgrounds manager—who stood patiently in his corral watching the crowds file through to the arena. Don Lupo with his Stan Kenton sweatshirt. The half-finished "Roman Ruin" of the new arena, the empty vodka jug and the broken bongo lying in the grass Monday morning. That was Monterey 1962.

The 1963 Jazz Festival

Dizzy Gillespie selling the NAACP Equality Button on the mall . . .

. . . Miles Davis and Thelonious Monk embracing in the Hunt Club bar . . .

. . . Harry James and Miles Davis playing touch football with Dizzy Gillespie's horn backstage Sunday night while Gillespie complained "aw, come on fellas, gimme back my horn" . . .

. . . Jimmy Witherspoon's encore Sunday night after the lights went out and while the other trio was beginning to play . . .

. . . The look on Victor Sproles' face when he realized Witherspoon was singing with TWO trios accompanying him . . .

. . . John Lewis taking over on piano Sunday afternoon . . .

. . . Allen Ginsberg striding majestically down the center aisle Sunday afternoon, hair flowing in the wind . . .

. . . Steve McQueen grinning . . .

. . . Kim Novak paying $20 for one of Dizzy Gillespie's Equality pins . . .

. . . The startled looks people gave the Dizzy Gillespie for President banner . . .

. . . The guy with the beard selling programs . . .

. . . The real trumpets on the real chairs on the side stage which were used as decorations and hung in the air . . .

. . . Thelonious Monk arriving on-stage Saturday night wearing an overcoat and a hat . . .

. . . Roy Gaines' guitar accompaniment to Jimmy Witherspoon . . .

. . . The expression on the face of Sleepy Matsumoto (the tenor from Japan) when he came on stage with Gerry Mulligan and Jack Teagarden . . .

. . . Gerry Mulligan's lovely solo playing . . .

. . . Jon Hendricks singing "I Wonder What's Become of Sally" . . .

. . . George Tucker's bass playing on "Li'l Darlin'" . . .

. . . John Lewis filling in the answers for Minny Witherspoon's blues singing Sunday afternoon . . .

. . . Jimmy Lyons filling a stage wait with announcements Sunday night . . .

. . . Carmen McRae's fan on the north side of the arena who screamed out "sing it, baby" . . .

. . . The guy in shorts Saturday night . . .

. . . The people on the special bleachers at the rear . . .

. . . The metal sculpture of Dizzy Gillespie at the art show . . .

. . . Dizzy Gillespie signing autographs in unexpected places in the Hunt Room . . .

. . . The silence of the crowd during Jon Hendricks' announcement for Birmingham children . . .

. . . James Moody's solo on "I'm in the Mood for Love" . . .

. . . Gildo Mahones and Jimmy Smith's playing for Witherspoon's blues set . . .

. . . The horse that got out of the corral . . .

. . . The representatives of Hell's Angels . . .

. . . The bull fighter ballet at 2 a.m. on the mall with Miles Davis' agent, Ben Shapiro, playing the matador and his wife, Mickey Shapiro, the bull . . .

. . . The French jazz magazine editor . . .

. . . The photographer from the Japanese edition of *Down Beat* . . .

. . . Ruth Price tripping over a microphone cord after her solo with the Harry James band . . .

. . . The Dizzy Gillespie for President balloons floating down from the San Carlos Hotel Saturday morning . . .

. . . Charlie Rouse, eyes closed, on stage listening to Thelonious Monk's piano solo . . .

. . . John Hammond's intelligent, informative and articulate Saturday afternoon announcements . . .

. . . John Lewis removing a ladder from in front of the stage . . .

. . . Joe Sullivan's lovely ballad solo . . .

. . . Bassist Red Callender, who just came up to enjoy the festival and never played a note . . .

. . . The costumes of the Ghana drummers . . .

. . . The sign on the Casa Munras, "Weather Today: Lyon Hearted" . . .

. . . The traffic jam Saturday night . . .

. . . The absence of bongos on the grounds . . .

. . . Saxophonist Jimmy Woods in the Gerald Wilson band, encouraging Witherspoon Sunday afternoon . . .

. . . The two kids who sailed over the fence fully visible to everyone but the police who were looking in other directions . . .

. . . The omnipresent armed guards . . .

. . . Jon Hendricks' solo from the Miles Davis record of "Bye Bye Blackbird" . . .

. . . Miles smiling.

Jazz at Monterey – 1964

Gildo Mahones' lovely piano chords behind Roy Gaines' blues vocal (the lyrics were King Pleasure's from "Parker's Mood") on Saturday afternoon . . .

. . . Big Mama Willie Mae Thornton in the Hunt Club after the show . . .

. . . the cuffs on Duke Ellington's trousers: At least four inches high . . .

. . . the beautiful sound all weekend . . .

. . . Charlie Mingus smiling and signing autographs after the Sunday afternoon show . . .

. . . the blend of Johnny Hodges and Charlie Parker in the alto saxophone playing of Charles McPherson Sunday afternoon . . .

. . . Miles Davis saying he had to be back Sunday night for Dizzy Gillespie's set because "he stabs me, even in my sleep" . . .

. . . the music fans shushing the loud talkers during Mingus' performance . . .

. . . Milton Hunt disguised as Pancho Villa Sunday afternoon . . .

. . . Dizzy Gillespie, Jon Hendricks and Joe Williams singing with Big Mama Saturday afternoon and their exit with the curtains closing and Big Mama kicking out through them . . .

. . . Gerry Mulligan buying a plastic machine gun to shoot down the airplanes . . .

. . . Woody Herman's beautiful performance of "Blue Monk" . . .

. . . Bola Sete's red chair for his solo appearance . . .

. . . Buddy Collette saying what an inspiration it had been to play Monterey and to play Mingus' music . . .

. . . Al McKibbon smoking a huge B.C. (Before Castro) cigar . . .

. . . Kermit Scott, who played tenor with Thelonious Monk 20 years ago at Minton's Playhouse where bop was born, greeting Monk backstage . . .

. . . the swinging groove of Saturday afternoon's show . . .

. . . Vic Dickenson playing "Basin Street" Friday night . . .

. . . Miles Davis' agent, Ben Shapiro, dressed up to look like Peter Sellers complete with mustache . . .

. . . the list of politicians who asked for passes . . .

. . . Paul Vieregge's pampas grass stage decorations for the MJQ Saturday night . . .

. . . Jon Hendricks' new girl singer, Pat Harris, looking like a SNCC worker at a fund raising party . . .

. . . Carol Sloane's nose and Jon Hendricks' eye visible through the photographer's peep hole on the stage during the Ellington concert . . .

. . . Jake Hanna, Woody Herman's marvelous drummer, telling someone backstage, "I'm a visual drummer" . . .

. . . Gerry Mulligan closing the after-hours session with Mingus, John Lewis and himself saying, "We have to stop or Jimmy Lyons will get busted . . ."

. . . the weather, which was so warm Monk didn't have to wear his overcoat . . .

. . . the Vince Guaraldi cardboard mustaches and the Dizzy Gillespie buttons that were everywhere . . .

. . . Duke Ellington, in the oldest gag in the Ellington bag, holding the music for Johnny Hodges to read . . .

. . . the standing ovation at the end of Vince and Bola's performance . . .

. . . Mingus . . .

Trumpets Triumph – 1965

"The afternoons are our luxury," Jimmy Lyons, general manager of the Monterey Jazz Festival, said a couple of years ago, but the way it is now the afternoons are not only the luxury but the breadwinners as well.

Saturday afternoon's show was a sellout and yesterday's came close. Preliminary estimates indicate the festival will gross over $120,000 this year.

Trumpets were the theme this year and the festival opened Friday night with trumpets galore —Dizzy Gillespie, Harry Edison, Ray Copeland and Louis Armstrong. But on Saturday afternoon it was alto saxophonist John Handy III, violinist Mike White and pianist Denny Zeitlin's Trio that drew standing ovations.

Handy's set, which was midway in the Saturday afternoon, was a musical powerhouse. Playing his original compositions, "Spanish

Lady" and "If Only We Knew," Handy, in a long string of highly emotional passages, rose to climax after climax to draw applause from the crowd and the musicians. It was a personal triumph for the San Francisco State College saxophonist and for his virtuoso musicians—drummer Terry Clarke, bassist Don Thompson, violinist Mike White and guitarist Jerry Hahn. They produced one of the most musically satisfying performances of the festival's recent years.

Zeitlin's trio, which preceded Handy, was almost as successful. Drummer Jerry Granelli and bassist Charlie Haden worked out a series of intricate passages with blinding virtuosity and the crowd roared back its appreciation, especially on "Carnival," and gave them a standing ovation.

Saturday night, Duke Ellington, who didn't go on until after 10:30, kept the audience entranced with number after number until after 1, and never sounded better.

His new singer, Esther Merrill, a gospel voice from Detroit, sang the exquisite "Come Sunday" and two gospel-style numbers, all written by Ellington. She was superb. Her powerful voice brought the crowd to a high pitch of excitement.

Ellington followed this with another surprise, the appearance of the sensational tap dancer, Bunny Briggs. After opening with a fetching vocal version of "Tulip or Turnip," Briggs proceeded to demonstrate the fact that he is a member of the small, elite group of master dancers of jazz. He was visual (with "Applejack") and he was musical (with "David Danced") and completely knocked out the audience and the critics. I have never seen any public performance by a tap dancer as exciting as Briggs' appearance.

Then, just as one wondered what possibly could come next, Ellington turned loose a piano player, and baritonist Harry Carney, for "Satin Doll" and "Sophisticated Lady." Johnny Hodges earlier had gotten the crowd rocking with "Feeling Kinda Blue" and "Things Ain't What They Used To Be."

The Ellington program included "Ad Lib on Nippon" and several other numbers which, in the opinion of the band and other musicians and, I might add, my own, added up to one of the best Ellington performances in years. It ended with

Dizzy Gillespie, Clark Terry and Rex Stewart playing "Rockin' in Rhythm" with the band.

When the police curfew was gently enforced, Duke said "The police department wants you to know that it, too, loves you madly." The musicians in the audience did not want to quit, despite the hour, and Jon Hendricks and Dizzy Gillespie did a quick ad lib trumpet and vocal coda.

Earlier in the evening Clark Terry and Jon Hendricks did a wildly humorous vocal blues, "Mumbles," and Dizzy had played a hauntingly beautiful ballad, "My Funny Valentine" as well as a wildly swinging "Kush." Tomorrow I'll discuss some of the other events of the weekend, including the piano playing of Buster Bailey of the Louis Armstrong All Stars . . . and the singing, Friday night, of Mary Stallings as well as the curiously ambivalent performance Saturday of Charles Mingus, which ranged from deeply moving to bewilderingly frustrating.

The Fat Is Close to the Fire—1965

Improvisation is the soul of jazz and all that, but Duke Ellington maintains that the improvisatory element in jazz always has been overemphasized.

It certainly was at Monterey and it strikes me that the moment of truth for that marvelous festival is at hand. On Saturday night, Earl "Fatha" Hines stood backstage after the show had started (he was the third artist on the bill) and wondered who would play bass and drums with him.

It turned out that Jerry Granelli and John Heard were able to fill in. So Earl talked over his routines and arrangements before going on stage. Heard had worked with Hines back East so the territory was familiar to him.

It worked. First because the musicians are able to improvise and because Earl Hines is a remarkable soloist and a virtuoso pianist and showman. But it was unfair to Earl; he would have been better had he been able to have rehearsals and to plan what he was to do.

Throughout the weekend Jon Hendricks and Dizzy Gillespie filled in, ad libbing while stage changes were made, padding, padding, padding.

It was disgraceful that plans were not made so this sort of thing was unnecessary. And if the festival and its director, Jimmy Lyons, do not face up to this, Monterey may very well be in trouble. It's fat now and living on its reputation and the momentum of its great years. This year could easily have been a disaster; what saved it was the performances of the musicians. Not the planning. There was little of that.

Saturday afternoon was grossly mis-handled. The festival orchestra then, as on the other occasions it appeared under Gil Fuller's direction, obviously had not had the rehearsals it was supposed to have had prior to the festival. In fact the best things that orchestra did all weekend were ad lib blues. Russ Garcia's interminable movie music bit was unnecessary and a bore. This all left Mingus, who was supposed to have an hour and a half, starting later than 4:30.

Friday night was also sloppy. Rex Stewart's music was not rehearsed properly. And the trumpet theme, heralded in publicity and in the program, disintegrated. Clark Terry, Rex Stewart, Harry Edison and Henry "Red" Allen were all brought out, only to be wasted in the shows themselves. That was a thoughtless affront to these artists.

Although Ellington had indicated some time before the festival that tap dancer Bunny Briggs would appear with him, there was no stage space for Briggs' dance and Duke had to move microphones himself to make a small, inadequate space.

Otherwise, something that has been great and moving and a joy to all of us will go the way of all American institutions. The syndrome in this society is to build a better mousetrap and then find a way of cutting back while maintaining the volume. Let's not have that happen at Monterey.

The list is endless. Ethel Ennis was added to the Sunday night program because RCA Victor wanted to be represented and was, thus, not hired at her usual fee. Beware of record companies bearing gifts. No real attempt was made to get a substitute for Miles Davis. It turned out to be an exciting evening but no one expected it to be. Tjader didn't even have his set recorded, though it ended up being the hit of the night. He didn't think it would work out that way.

In its early days, Monterey had side benefits, little touches, buttons for the musicians who appeared; small but real steaks, cheap, at the stands. Now the steaks are pressed, frozen meat and musicians have only the stage applause for memories.

What this festival needs, and needs urgently, is a musical director. If John Lewis will not return and no substitute for him is found, we can expect worse afternoons than Sunday's tawdry show. The festival sound was not as good this year as formerly. The usher system collapsed nightly at the end of the shows and there were numerous small signs of decay.

An agonizing reappraisal is needed if Monterey is to maintain its stature as America's best jazz festival. And first and foremost on the list of things to be done is to put someone musicians respect and will obey and who has a capacity for hard work and a head for planning in charge of the musical programming. If not John Lewis, then J. J. Johnson.

Remembrance of a Festival Past–1966

Memories of Monterey: the beautiful girl with the black and orange feathered hat . . . the barefooted drummer with Don Ellis . . . Gil Evans' black and white checked suit with the long vents in the coat . . . Big Mama Thornton posing . . . "Big Mama Thornton for Governor" banner Sunday afternoon . . . Consigne Anderson feeding her baby at the rehearsal hall Saturday morning.

Muddy Waters' little dance during "I Got My Mojo Workin'" . . . Big Black, eyes closed, listening to the other players . . . the guy backstage with the tape recorder playing loudly at all times . . . the chick in the wild sun hat, a bucket shaped affair of blue cellophane with a white bottom . . . Gil Evans listening to Bola Sete . . . the musicians fascinated by Palhino's special drum effects . . . Big Mama's gold dress.

The microphone hanging over the tuba in Gil Evans' band . . . the quick curtain . . . Ray Brown's all too brief appearances . . . Jon Hendricks' line about Big Mama—"She's been playin' in clubs in the Bay Area, where you been?" . . . Duke Ellington, Bunny Briggs and Tony Watkins posing as the airplane flew overhead . . . Howard Johnson's tuba solos with Gil Evans . . . the white drawings of Sambo in Sambo's . . . the traffic jam.

Mike Bloomfield and Elvin Bishop of the Paul Butterfield Band mesmerized by Big Mama's singing at the Saturday morning rehearsal . . . Jerry Hahn scampering off stage for another guitar string Sunday afternoon . . . Gil Evans standing with arms outstretched at the end of a number . . . the crowd around Carmen McRae in the Hunt Club . . . Sam Woodyard's solo on "La Plus Belle Africaine" playing with his hands on the drums.

The topless dancer (male) Saturday afternoon . . . the cop who sweet-talked the hostile drunk out of the arena Saturday night without laying a hand on him . . . the guitar players on the lawn by the administration building . . . the Dizzy Gillespie sweatshirts and buttons and the balloons (released by some undisciplined brats—mine) Sunday afternoon . . . Herbie Henderson's red coat . . . Charles Lloyd's beads and sandals . . . Jack Casady, bassist of the Jefferson Airplane, staying down for the rest of the festival saying "I'm a jazz fan."

Jimmy Lyons, exhausted as always by festival time, trying to ad lib bright fill-ins while stage sets were changed . . . the empty seats Monday morning looking lonesome after the festival . . . Red Callender, Buddy Collette, Plas Johnson and other Hollywood musicians up for fun and not to perform . . . Wally Heider sitting majestically in [the]sound truck backstage watching the entire affair on a tiny TV screen . . . the lovely girl photographer from Chicago.

The parties with the portable beer kegs Sunday afternoon . . . the traffic jam . . . the girl with the backless dress in the Hunt Club . . . the clusters of picnickers after the afternoon show . . . the kids asking Big Mama for her autograph . . . the flash cubes popping all night long . . . John Hammond introducing Count Basie—a moment of jazz history . . . Vince Guaraldi's mustachios, dark glasses, and gaucho hat.

Memories of a Jazz Festival–1967

Memories of the Monterey Jazz Festival: the guy in the huge straw sombrero with "Jazz—can you dig it?" scrawled on it. Not if I'm sitting behind you, baby . . . the man with the copy of the encyclopedia of jazz on his lap checking the names and numbers . . . the line of campers on the road by the fairgrounds, set for the weekend and some of them never moved even to go in to the show . . . the costume changes of the lady photographer from Chicago . . . Ornette Coleman's suits—one black and white chessboard check and one black and gold brocade—"Ornate" Coleman, Bucky McGeoghan of Pan Am called him.

John Lewis' introductions Sunday afternoon . . . the TV cameraman in the crows-nest who started swinging to Woody Herman and almost ruined the closed circuit TV . . . John Handy in a sun helmet and Bermuda shorts . . . the Dionysiac crowds dancing in the aisles . . . the Woody Herman band packed into the sound booth under the stage after the festival listening to the playback of the Bill Holman composition.

Sound engineer Wally Heider saying, as Ray Brown started to play with Carmen McRae, "Ray Brown would sound good if you put a telephone in front of him . . ." . . . Don Pruitt's wild "Work Song" pants . . . Janis Joplin on stage Saturday afternoon hitching up her pants and then saying the magic word over the mike . . . Dizzy Gillespie squatting on stage to listen to Carmen McRae, then backstage later telling her how great she was . . .

Headlights' light show films . . . Columbia executive John Hammond in a photographer's hat . . . the airplane that flew over Saturday afternoon while Big Brother was playing and sounded like a reverberator . . . the gal with the Malcolm X sweat-shirt . . . the beautiful blonde in a slender bra, a tiny bikini and mammoth press badge on her tummy . . . Illinois H. Jacquet playing the bassoon . . . John Lewis rehearsing the violinists . . . Richie Havens beaming backstage.

The kids sleeping out on the lawn . . . Dizzy, Ray Brown and Louis Bellson played softly backstage . . . festival president Mel Isenberger inspecting the grounds from a golf cart . . . the European musicians digging the scene . . . the guy with the button reading "The Viet Cong Never

Called Me a Nigger" . . . the girl in the tight silver pants and the Indian headband and feather getting a double take from Dizzy as she walked down the aisle . . . Woody Herman's grandchildren sound asleep in the stands during Woody's set.

Stagehand Dave Topelis who hitchhikes from Florida, Arizona and other points each year to work at the festival, getting his kicks playing Louis Bellson's drums at one ayem on a flat bed truck which was moving them from the stage area to the rehearsal hall . . . the relaxed ushers and the cops and the noisiest audience in years. The guy behind me who only shut up when Big Brother was playing . . . the balloons going up from the stadium filled with helium . . . the European musicians at the La Playa hotel . . . the East Bay Dragon and The Chosen Few riding their hogs down Fremont with a police escort.

The amplifier-hugging, guitar-smashing finale to the Big Brother number . . . RCA Victor's Steve Sholes and Brad McCuen, each 300 pounds, and Wally Heider (another heavyweight) looking like the Chicago Bears 1940 line . . . Woody Herman's 12-inch coat vents . . . the lights in Gil Melle's show . . . the Clara Ward Gospel Singers slow version of "When the Saints Go Marching In" . . .

Jimmy Lyons' eyes filling with tears when he was interviewed for TV backstage . . . Percy Heath warming up playing the bass under the stage . . . the photographers swarming around Dizzy and Carmen when they embraced backstage . . . Dizzy Gillespie's introduction to Franco Ambrosetti . . . the longhaired stage hands.

The boy-meets-girl introductions on the grounds. "My name's Ray, what's yours?" . . . Illinois Jacquet in the Hunt Club announcing he was staying over an extra day . . . Earl Hines' beautiful daughters . . . the European musicians arriving at the airport for their first glimpse of Monterey . . . Dizzy Gillespie being wired for sound so the camera crew for "The Telephone Hour" could follow him around . . . the press corps with its festival briefcases.

Earl Hines losing his pipe backstage . . . Carmen McRae calling Ray Brown "the greatest bass player in the world" . . . John Lewis madly searching for a pencil sharpener during rehearsal . . . the dancing of the Clara Ward singers . . . the wiggling of Ray Nance.

Next Time, Music Before Money– 1968

The Monterey Jazz Festival attendance and box office gross this year was up over last and may, when all the returns are in, be the biggest in its 11-year history.

But the Festival is in serious trouble with both the fans and the musicians over the bad management and poor coordination and planning which resulted in the fiasco of the first three concerts this year in which the sound system finally went dead altogether.

The problems involved in Monterey are serious ones and they are vital not only to this festival but to the entire jazz world.

The jazz festivals have been an important area for jazz musicians, increasingly so in recent years when they have provided an opportunity for many kinds of jazz music to be heard and for many jazz artists to be exposed to a wider spectrum of the potential audience than they would ordinarily have access to.

Monterey's role in all of this has been particularly important.

The Monterey Jazz Festival came on the scene after the Newport Festival, and its success, based on an adventuresome programming policy, a dedication to the artist and the music and a willingness to present both the old and the new, caused Newport to revise its policies. There is no doubt of this. Jazz musicians loved Monterey because they were well treated there and allowed to play their music as they wished. Jazz fans loved it, not only for the beautiful setting, but for the interesting and unusual programs it presented.

But as Newport has grown more progressive, Monterey has grown more stuffy and cautious and conservative.

Everyone connected with the Festival works hard. That goes without saying, really. But I suspect that the Board and the General Manager are not always talking about the same things.

The Festival is only as important as the music. The artists make the music, therefore "artist" should be the most important word at Monterey. And there are times when "artist" seems to mean "employee."

The checks and balances set by the Board in its contract with the General Manager are intended to keep him from becoming reckless with money.

Yet this laudatory plan actually serves as an incentive to cut corners so that the net profit will be greater. It is paradoxical.

No one expects the Board to program the Festival and to attend other festivals and audition new and old groups in performance at clubs and other festivals. That's what the General Manager ought to do. But this does not happen. And I am convinced that one of the reasons for Monterey's recent failures to live up to its well publicized reputation for musical integrity is that the General Manager does not go to other festivals nor to clubs to see the groups. The determined attention to re-runs implies a lack of knowledge of what is happening now.

Monterey also sadly needs someone to coordinate detail behind the scenes. Part of the sound problem resulted from a rehearsal snafu because the Count Basie band did not know there was a rehearsal. This failure to communicate is inexcusable and responsibility rests on the Festival, not on Basie or his managers.

John Lewis is widely publicized as the musical director and/or consultant. I bow to no one in my admiration for Mr. Lewis' talents as a pianist, composer and musical director of the Modern Jazz Quartet. But as far as Monterey is concerned, either he should actually insist that he be consulted (as he has been in the past) or he should not accept the title. As it is, he is used as a cover for what goes on. The failure to book any of the younger, experimental jazz players, such as Albert Ayler, Cecil Taylor, Archie Shepp, etc., has been attributed to a dictum by Lewis which he denies he ever issued.

In the days when Monterey's main concern was music, the ludicrous appearance of a politician on one night and a committee from the American Federation of Musicians on another to read boring official commendations to the Festival and the General Manager would not have been tolerated. Accept them, though we all know it's a shuck, but don't let them on stage. It's an offense to the music.

At this point Monterey is at a dead end. New jazz doesn't just mean youngsters playing in standard styles, no matter how proficient they may be. The whole concept of this Festival should be reexamined, as its good will is draining away. Critics from the East simply did not attend this year. As one wrote me, "There's nothing on the program I haven't heard before."

Where are the new groups? More of them appear at the Both-And than at the Monterey Jazz Festival. Freddie Hubbard, who was at the Both-And, would have been an asset at Monterey, and the real avant garde simply is not recognized. Nor, I might add, is the cadre of surviving old timers such as the Preservation Hall Jazz Band.

It pains me to go into all this because I love the Monterey Jazz Festival. But if it doesn't change its course, it will become just another weekend for a booze bust-out.

Excursions in nostalgia are all right and there is nothing wrong with the standard performers. Some of them are truly great. But it is high time Monterey reconsidered its safe course. At the moment it is making money, but I suggest that the jazz musicians and the fans themselves will turn against it solidly if it doesn't do more than that.

Music, not money, should be the first concern of a music festival.

High Spots at Monterey–1969

Now ineluctably headed down the road from festival to carnival, its programming witless and insensitive, its sound erratic, the Monterey Jazz Festival this weekend nevertheless had moments of glory.

There was Little Esther Phillips' magnificent set Saturday afternoon. There was Tony Williams' hurricane of sound Friday night, and there was Miles Davis' eloquent, sweet and utterly musical performance Saturday night which was the Festival's creative highlight.

Little Esther, new to Monterey and to most of the audience, has been known mainly in rhythm and blues. But she turned out to be a jazz singer in the purest sense of the term. She immediately won the audience when she opened singing King Pleasure's lyrics to "Moody Mood for Love." She gave the words another dimension entirely by making it a sexy love song and really hitting the audience with it. She sang the Beatles' "And I Love Him" and ended with a great blues, "I Got a Cold, Cold Feelin'." Bobby Bryant's Festival band accompanied her expertly and with great feeling. The result was not only a surprise but a pleasure.

Friday night's opening concert began with a pointless set by Peanuts Hucko, a clarinetist, which was adored by those in the audience who define jazz in terms of Las Vegas lounges and Pete Fountain. It is a wonder this kind of thing has survived'at all. Louise Tobin was brought on to sing. I had not heard of her since Harry James divorced her to marry Betty Grable 30 years ago. Red Norvo, a really interesting musician, carried whatever weight there was. It is sad to see him surrounded by such mediocrity.

The Modern Jazz Quartet, disadvantageously programmed, still played very well (when the sound allowed them to be heard) and Jean-Luc Ponty, the brilliant violinist, joined them for two John Lewis compositions. Four jets interrupted the MJQ's set.

Tony Williams' new group presented the astonishing percussionist with Larry Young on organ and John McLaughlin on guitar. The sound worked for this group and though their music is difficult to absorb, they got to the audience and played exceptionally well. It is a completely new sound in jazz, an amalgam of electronic volume and percussion that is dissonant and sinewy and can be overwhelming.

Sly and the Family Stone, who ended Friday night's show, is an extremely visual act. They came on stage dressed in space age costumes, and backed by more amplifiers than Roger Calkins has sold in five years. Midway in their first number, they split, and a long pause ensued in which negotiations were conducted. Eventually the group returned. A missing piano stool had been found, it turned out. Then Sly wailed out a wild set including his hits, which really turned the audience on. They are a great show.

Saturday afternoon belonged to Little Esther and to Buddy Guy, the blues singer and guitarist. Guy and his small group were as tight as a gnat's rectum and they socked the blues to the audience, a group of tunes ranging from "Fever" to "Sweet Little Sixteen" that brought it all back home.

Roberta Flack, a new singer with a good future, sang a set with warmth and dexterity, and Lighthouse, a Canadian rock group, closed the afternoon. Both acts then appeared on the evening show, doing the same thing they did in the afternoon, a programming tour de force that boggled the mind.

However, Saturday night gave us both Miles and Monk. Davis now has Jack DeJohnette on

drums along with pianist Chick Corea, bassist Dave Holland and tenor Wayne Shorter. The latter doubles on soprano and Corea plays electric piano. The group's performance is continuous now; no pauses between numbers, one continual work. Saturday night Miles played brilliantly. His open horn tones were strong and full, sailing out over the audience. At one point he turned away from the microphone and could still be clearly heard, the fullness and purity of his tone carrying through the air. Shorter's performance on soprano was unusual, a distinct surprise and highly effective.

DeJohnette fits perfectly into this group, adding a remarkable new set of sounds to what is played by the horns. Corea suffered mechanical problems with the piano, so that it did not function at its best and was only a tantalizing hint of what he can do.

Monk's set, both with the quartet and with Bryant's big band, was pure Monk—humorous, sparse lines flowing into a pulsating rhythm. Charlie Rouse played his tenor solos absolutely beautifully, their form and his sound merging perfectly.

The Monterey crowd was its usual marvelous mixture, many of them juiced out of their skulls and chattering like magpies. Fremont Street's line of campers and caravans was an extravagant assortment of life styles, gypsy, Four-H Club, and Arlo Guthrie. In time it will resemble not Woodstock but Ghengis Khan's encampment at Lhasa.

Sour Notes at Jazz Festival–1971

One of the things that people have been talking about ever since the Monterey Jazz Festival last month was the excessive drinking. The audience was awash in a sea of booze that resembled nothing so much as the old Kezar convention of bar-room excursion bus parties at a football game.

The audience was so crocked that those who wanted to hear Carmen McRae on Saturday night had to turn around and shush the juice-heads into some kind of uneasy quiet.

The implications are inescapable, I think. Monterey has degenerated into a three-day, free-form bash which has had increasingly little to do with actual music.

It has been some time since anything new and-or unusual musically has been presented at Monterey. Gimmickery has been substituted for innovation and when an afternoon show is composed of student bands, it's no wonder the audience gets drunk at those prices.

Actually I think that the reason everybody gets so juiced at Monterey these days is boredom. If the music was interesting enough, there might be less reason to get smashed. But the music for some time now has been, with precious few exceptions, the mixture as before. Familiarity and safety in an art form that is by definition experimental.

The Monterey management is actually out of touch with what jazz is all about these days and out of touch with the sound and the people who are creating it.

There are dozens of first rate musicians and groups whose music is exciting and interesting and innovative and who are being greeted now in Europe (if not in Monterey) in exactly the same way the innovators of the '40s were. Jazz, like everything else, is repeating its history.

Jazz is the music of black America and it doesn't alter anything to get mad at me for saying that. It is a simple obvious statement of truth. Black Americans invented it, set the styles on every instrument and with every kind of group, and they still dominate, with a lonely few exceptions, the ranks of those musicians whose playing affects the jazz music of the world.

Yet the school bands on stage at Monterey were lily white. As the audience for the festival has grown blacker over the years, the stage has grown whiter. It is a curious situation and one which I suspect is going to bring objections on the part of the black community.

The Monterey management seems to be under the impression that Dionne Warwicke and Roberta Flack are both agents provocateur, not to be booked because they may spark riots, an equation which seems to parallel Attica official reasoning.

Actually, it is only the latest example of just how far from the reality of today's black jazz music the Monterey Jazz Festival management actually is. They apparently do not know who these people are.

Monterey was for many years the realization of a dream of many people who felt that jazz was not being given its due in this society (it still is not) and that somehow by bringing together the best of the new and the old, the familiar and the experimental in the music, the audiences and the musicians themselves would all benefit, as would the music.

In many ways it worked. It certainly worked for some time. Monterey's example changed the Newport Festival, for one (which had spawned Monterey in the first place). It gave new careers to old timers who had all but disappeared, and it provided springboards for new talent to make its mark.

But that is not what happens any longer. Monterey is now programmed so safely, so carefully and so stingily that there is no room for anything but an occasional good performance. No longer does Monterey solicit ideas for programs like the "Evolution of the Blues" or "The Real Ambassadors," the kind of thing which could never be seen or heard anywhere else.

All that happens at Monterey now is a succession of five concerts jammed into one weekend and the knowledge that because everybody is staying over Saturday night the Sunday afternoon show can be staged with less regard for its box office weight. That's all.

Erroll Garner made his debut at Monterey this year. That's nice and he was excellent. But what he did one could have seen and heard at Concord. Great as he is, Garner might have been enticed into some situation with, say, Earl Hines that could have produced a historic evening.

But no historic evenings are going to be produced at Monterey as long as the festival insists on aping the kind of American success story wherein a good product is launched and made successful and then becomes an exercise in how far it can be cut back for the same money.

At this point in time, Monterey is being programmed from a position of fear. John Lewis, the musical director, apparently fears jazz is dying and must depend for box office success on tried and true names.

Jimmy Lyons, the general manager, apparently fears booking the young, new black musicians will result in riots. The city of Monterey wishes the festival would dry up and blow away and then there would not be the inundation of blacks and weirdos each September.

I don't know what the future will bring or what it can bring. Perhaps there is no solution.

On one of the concerts, Clark Terry, Dizzy Gillespie, Roy Eldridge and one of the young students from the stage bands played a tribute to Louis Armstrong. It was nice and it had its point and Roy's solo was exquisite, by far the most moving music I heard all weekend.

But the young man who came from the stage band was acutely embarrassed and obviously felt he didn't belong. And, with all kindness towards him, he didn't belong, and the management was really out of its mind to have him there. He may, if he stays in jazz, develop to a point where he WILL belong, but this was a tribute to a great artist at the end of the summer in which he died, to a man who in a very real artistic sense was the father of all the music presented that weekend.

It was a terrible position to put that young man into and it demonstrated dramatically how little artistic thought goes into Monterey these days.

Monterey is currently enjoying financial prosperity. The first three concerts sold out and the other two were heavily attended. It has international stature now and people come from all over the world to it.

But I am convinced this will not last unless the caliber of the programs for the weekend rises. Unless Monterey brings to its audiences something special, there is really no other reason to go down there than to spend the weekend getting smashed with your friends. And you can do that at home.

Oddly enough, the weekend that Monterey was so boring, various Russian cities were being treated to new, unusual and exquisite jazz music. Duke Ellington was there.

No More Spark–1972

Back in the mid fifties when the jazz festival idea was being started in this country, first at Newport and then at Monterey, jazz was available in live performance mostly in night clubs.

The night club had been the staple of jazz employment for a long time, emerging as a specialized place from the general entertainment club or the black/white club of the '30s.

The basic motivation behind the jazz festivals was two-fold. Part of it was to bring jazz out into the sunlight and make it available in the kind of family-style outdoors picnic, Stern Grove kind of environment. European music festivals had been in operation for generations and there already existed at the time several European jazz festivals.

But also in the thrust was another factor. Jazz had moved into the concert hall with some regularity in the 1950s and there was a drive to find it other locations. Implicit in this was the jazz musician's own drive for respectability, the right to appear in as good a venue as other artists appeared in.

I wonder about all this now after the most recent Monterey Jazz Festival. Perhaps, the time is ripe for a swing back to the raunchy jazz club. At least if you want to hear interesting, exciting music.

The basic operative law for any concert, festival or film event involving music is that it is precisely as good as the music. No amount of frills can save it and if the music is good enough, the most depressing environment becomes inspirational. The Black Hawk proved that to any regular patron.

At Monterey this year the stage was decorated and lit better than it has been in years. But what transpired on it was for me and many others depressing.

Basically it's just a job now to most of the musicians. A welcome job, but a job nonetheless. There is little more than the spark picked up from other musicians. There is no spark from the audience, it's too drunk.

The acts are programmed like a series of night club events with no real thought as to contrast, or order of presentation. To open the festival with the avant-garde (a dreary avant-garde at that) music of Elvin Jones was a programming disaster embarrassing to a high school junior prom manager.

But there is a great deal more than this troubling me in the fall-out from Monterey. As it now is constituted, the festival is committed to the rotating use of an ever diminishing group of artists which can be expected in a few more years to have all but died off.

There is no room for experimentation; no room for innovation. The festival which presented Ornette Coleman and John Coltrane on an afternoon performance illustrating a lecture on avant-garde music by Gunther Schuller and filled the arena, now gives us summer re-runs of old familiar favorites. Oldies but goodies—and not so goodies.

For the serious jazz listener, there is no longer any reason to go to Monterey. In the past, one of its chief attractions was the fact that it would present musical events impossible to see any other time. This is no longer true, as witness the recent programs.

Although the other festivals, especially the European ones on which Monterey was based, include plenty of picnics and parties, they are apparently still basically for people who want to listen to music. Monterey is now a musical background for a host of booze busts and it makes almost no difference who is on stage. It might be possible just to show films of old festivals. How would the drunks know?

It is a sad thing, like the sight of an aging hipster, to see Monterey lose its creativity. It has been an important festival in a national and international sense. It simply is not any longer. It changed the U. S. concert scene, and shook up Newport so deeply by its success that Newport changed. But now Monterey merely searches to recreate moments from its own past.

Of course there are individual moments of beauty. There are still great artists doing the thing they created and only suffering because they are placed in a banal situation by myopic programming. Eddie Vinson, Joe Williams, Sonny Stitt, Roy Eldridge are a few of those who triumphed in that sense.

Since it is obvious that the prejudices of the authorities at Monterey will prevent any truly experimental music being heard there again, what is there to do? I have only one suggestion.

Unless they wish to drive the audience back into the booze joints where, at least, you can get close enough to the music to be enveloped in its feeling, they will have to think. What the thinking should produce, I believe, is carefully organized and planned and rehearsed pageants and programs for the evening and afternoon concerts which will utilize the elements available (groups, bands, singers) and arrange them in some kind of order and with some kind of theme.

The highlights from Monterey's 15-year history are those programs which were planned and organized and worked on. The same formula will pay off artistically in the future as it has in the past.

Unless this is done, I see Monterey's profile shrinking even more as far as artistry goes. It will continue to be successful at the box office (and its organization can laugh, like Liberace, as they go to the bank) because the Monterey Peninsula is a great place to arrange for a social convention for groups from L. A. and the Bay Area to get together and party for three days. But musically it is now as predictable as a Nixon speech.

It's curious how it all ties together. When Monterey was artistically important, its patrons were the most amazingly creative sight on the planet. The costumes were a show in themselves. They are now dull.

Except for one young man whose sign on his hat read, "Wanted: Tickets for Sunday night's show; inquire within," there wasn't much more than you might expect on a Monterey street on a warm lunch hour.

It may really be that the jazz festival time is past and that the music itself will have to be presented now in concert halls and other interior scenes, with some smaller outdoor events. The recent Newport-at-New-York festival seems to indicate that.

And George Wein, who presented it as he has all the other Newport Festivals, is coming to the Bay Area in the late spring or early summer of next year with a three-or-four-day festival which will be spread all over with events in San Francisco, Oakland and Berkeley. I don't know how that will go, it depends on the planning I expect, but at least it is an interesting idea.

As it stands now, the verdict of a lady with whom I am acquainted strikes me as the best summary of the Monterey weekend. She came down this year and spent all her time in the Hunt Room sipping cocktails and watching the concerts on the closed circuit TV monitor. She says the only thing she missed was Willie Brown selling tickets at the box office.

It's a shame she missed that. As far as I was concerned, it was the best performance at the festival.

A 1971 jam session; left to right: Louis Bellson, Ray Brown, Mundell Lowe, Clark Terry, Roy Eldridge, Zoot Sims, Bill Harris, Eddie "Lockjaw" Davis, Benny Carter, John Lewis (piano)

Assessing the Festival

by Leonard Feather

The fourth annual Monterey Jazz Festival last weekend was a resounding success—artistically and financially. In a year that has seen the jazz-extravaganza phenomenon skidding toward esthetic confusion and financial disaster, it was the major reassurance of the season.

The five concerts (three evenings, two matinees) attracted 27,950 attentive and never over-demonstrative fans who paid $104,800 to hear some of the best, newest and freshest playing and writing ever created by America's liveliest art.

Four artists emerged with the bulk of the credit. They were J.J. Johnson, the composer and trombonist; John Birks (Dizzy) Gillespie, composer and trumpeter; Lalo Schifrin, 28-year-old Argentine composer and pianist with Gillespie's group; and Gunther Schuller, who conducted the large brass ensemble at the most important of the five concerts, the matinee featuring works by Johnson, Gillespie and Schifrin.

A fifth artist covered himself with an odd mixture of glory and verbiage. Duke Ellington, leader of what remains after 30 years the greatest big band in jazz, managed through a series of performances that presented his music and soloists at optimum level to compensate for a few regrettable lapses.

Duke was selected to act as master of ceremonies for the entire festival. Since he lives in the circumscribed world of his own music and rarely listens to that of others, he was at a loss to introduce his contemporaries knowledgeably and with an air of convincing authority. Patronizingly flippant and disarmingly charming by turns, he filled some of the lulls by playing piano solos at the side of the stage while the next act was being set up.

The opening show on Friday night, which attracted the smallest audience (4,200) was also the weakest musically though there were some admirable moments. These were provided mainly by Terry Gibbs' big band, with the vibraphonist leader driving his team or leading Hollywood musicians through a series of swinging arrangements by Bill Holman, Al Cohn and others.

A so-called "modern mainstream" set brought together a star-rich but disorganized group of soloists. Highlights of this set were "Russian Lullaby" and a blues, played by Dizzy Gillespie and the veteran violinist Stuff Smith; and a couple of tunes that brought together for the first time the two greatest jazz fiddlers, Stuff Smith and Ray Nance.

In other numbers, the talents of men like Ben Webster and Harry Carney were largely wasted and the attempt to form a vocal team out of Jimmy Rushing and Big Miller, backed by his band, proved that two 300-pound singers make far less than 600 pounds of blues.

The Saturday matinee was given over entirely to a show called "Ellington Carte Blanche," for which Duke was expected to come up with all kinds of innovations and surprises. But Duke goofed. The only new works played were a few inconsequential but pleasant pieces linked under the generic title, "The Girls," in four movements subtitled "Sarah," "Lena," "Mahalia," and "Dinah."

But there was so much superb, typical, timeless Ellington music, both at this performance and in the Sunday night show when the band closed the festival, that it would be unfair to carp. (Nevertheless I MUST carp at the inclusion of a nondescript male singer whom Duke prevailed upon to sing the same dull song at two shows.)

Dizzy Gillespie's fantastic musicianship, vitality and humor (AND his welcome vocal reunion with his alumnus Joe Carroll) dominated the show that played to a sellout house on Saturday night.

J.J. Johnson played three splendid numbers backed by a brass choir, but his tour de force was saved for the next day's matinee, when Gillespie was heard in "Perceptions," the world premiere of a work he commissioned Johnson to write.

Like the two other long works in the same program—Schifrin's "Gillespiana Suite" and the "Tunisian Fantasy" by Schifrin and Gillespie—Johnson's complex, partly atonal and consistently intriguing work showed impressively how fast the lines between classical music and jazz are disappearing. Schifrin and Johnson must now be ranked among the handful of composers fully equipped to fuse both streams successfully.

There were other attractions. Carmen McRae sang songs superbly and Odetta sang blues a little uncomfortably. The George Shearing and Dave Brubeck combos offered the mixture as usual.

Whatever faults there were at Monterey could be discounted as minor aberrations. The whole picture was one of valid music in an ideal setting. As one contented listener remarked: "This is the best place in the world to hold a jazz festival!"

The comment was significant when you consider the source, for it was made by George Wein, founder of the Newport Jazz Festival.

When Macy's endorses Gimbel's, you know he can't be kidding.

Valley Times, 1961
San Fernando Valley

J.J. Johnson, 1961

An American Salzburg

by Grover Sales

A few years ago, jazz festivals blossomed on the national scene like watermelons in the summertime. Led by Newport, the original and Big Daddy of all jazz festivals, an overpowering assemblage of "name" attractions, sometimes costing well over $100,000, would be offered during the weekends in Chicago, French Lick, Boston, Randall's Island, Detroit and Hollywood. On a smaller scale, any promoter who could sign up a few acts such as Louis Armstrong and Miles Davis for two days in Great Falls, Montana, had himself a "jazz festival." Nowhere was the end in sight.

Critical rumblings from the country's top jazz writers have assumed fearful proportions. Why go to the trouble of flying Dizzy Gillespie and Duke Ellington from New York to Hollywood and cut them off after twenty minutes on stage to make room for the next "name" in a seemingly endless cortege of jazz personalities? Jazz purists complained that, in order to lure the widest possible audience, non-jazz attractions like the Kingston Trio and Pat Suzuki were signed to buttress the already swollen programs. The most serious blot was the unruliness of the college crowds that flocked to Newport, beer cans in hand, for an unbridled weekend saturnalia. With the eruption on last year's July Fourth, aptly termed the "Newport Riot," national jazz fetes came in for an "agonizing reappraisal." Today, the festivals have dwindled down to a precious few—gone are the festivals at Hollywood Bowl, Great South Bay and Chicago. The French Lick Festival, which was moved to Evansville, Indiana, attracted a mere 1200 people over last June 16 weekend. Newport has changed its name and is offering an unbelievable lineup costing over six figures—including such stellar jazz luminaries as Judy Garland and Bob Hope.

And then, of course, there is Monterey.

Since the first Monterey Jazz Festival was held in 1958, it became obvious to all that this was to be no "festival" in the customary misuse of that word. Within three years, this rather modest venture with its limited budget and subdued atmosphere was being hailed by critics and musicians as an "American Salzburg."

"Monterey," wrote [the] *Chronicle*'s Ralph J. Gleason in his nationally syndicated column, "is a well-rounded presentation by musicians to attract music lovers, not by promoters to draw celebrants." *Time*, the Frankfurter *Zeitung* and the London *Times* were among the legions who were extravagant in their praise.

With the fourth annual Monterey Jazz Festival, September 22–23–24, promising to be the best attended on the basis of advance season ticket sales, we asked the festival's founder and manager Jimmy Lyons for some special comments on his brainchild, and why it had been singled out as **the** jazz festival. With a characteristic offhandedness and unstudied insouciance that has made Lyons the most popular jazz D.J. in the West, he replied: "Well, first of all, the festival is in Monterey. How can you beat Monterey as a festival site? The weather is idyllic, if not downright groovy, the scenery is a complete gas, and the entire atmosphere is **festive** in a very real sense. I can't describe it to anyone who hasn't been to a festival; all I know is, I've seen hung-up musicians relaxed in Monterey who have never been relaxed before in their frenetic lives.

"You might say Monterey compares to Newport as a small budget 'art' film compares to a super extravaganza like 'Ben Hur.' Perhaps the low budget is a blessing in disguise. In many ways it forces us to concentrate on the unusual and original, rather than merely to fling a lot of expensive talent on the stage.

"This fall, for example, the two great innovators in jazz, Duke Ellington and Dizzy Gillespie, each have an afternoon program entirely to themselves. In fact, we are calling the Saturday afternoon show 'Ellington Carte Blanche.' We don't even know what Duke intends to do, and it doesn't occur to me to ask.

"Every year we present music specially composed for Monterey that cannot be heard elsewhere. What's the sense of paying $7000 for Ella Fitzgerald, great as she is? You can hear Ella at the Fairmont Hotel, and for the same amount we can put on the 'Evolution of the Blues Song,' the big hit of last year's festival, and have enough loot left over to commission Ellington to write 'Suite Thursday.'"

San Francisco Town and Country
September, 1961

Grover Sales was Public Relations Director of the Monterey Jazz Festival, 1958–1964.

Duke Ellington rehearsing his "Suite Thursday" at the 1964 Monterey Festival.

The Festival Must Grow up

by Richard Hadlock

Now that the dust has settled in the big arena where Monterey's seventh annual jazz festival was staged two weeks ago, it might be a good time to ask a few questions about the future of this important musical event.

The Monterey Jazz Festival is a successful show. There is much good music, the grounds are attractive and the box office take now stacks up comfortably on the black side of the ledger. Yet, in some ways Monterey has failed to mature or to fulfill the promise that illuminated its early programs four or five years ago.

For one thing, there has been too much musical inbreeding over these six years. Pianist-composer John Lewis, billed since 1959 as the man who controls "all programming and selection of performing artists," has contributed a number of excellent performances, ideas and artist contacts.

But Lewis' circle of influence is relatively small in the enormous world of jazz. Since 1958 we have heard a good deal from friends of Lewis such as Gunther Schuller, J.J.Johnson, the Modern Jazz Quartet and Dizzy Gillespie. What of the dozens upon dozens of "outside" musicians who deserve to be heard? What of Gil Evans, Eddie Sauter, Bill Russo, Rod Leavitt, Clare Fischer and San Francisco's own John Handy, to point out only a few of the many outstanding composers currently seeking a platform?

Lewis did bring us Ornette Coleman, but what happened to the other avant garde jazzmen? Why hasn't Monterey sought out young explorers like Cecil Taylor, George Russell, Don Ellis, Ken McIntyre, Paul Bley or Larry Austin? It can't be a question of money, for some of these men would be delighted to appear for flat scale prices.

When the festival did take a chance on a new name, trumpeter Ted Curson, he was relegated to the small between-act stage and hardly noticed at all.

Similarly, Monterey has failed to do well by the old timers in jazz. There are, for instance, only a few genuine New Orleans marching band musicians left, but those who survive could stop the show at Monterey—and do it for minimum prices.

Why, you may wonder, should the festival care about these things, so long as the music is good and lots of people turn out? Here is why: the Monterey Jazz Festival has created for itself the image of a very special enterprise that "avoids the hackneyed and the trite" and "introduces important new artists rather than merely 'play it safe.'" I am quoting from the festival's own Statement of Policy.

In 1963 Monterey even enlarged its Policy, as follows: "The Monterey Jazz Festival is a serious musical presentation, whose main concern is with the individual freedom of the artist. Jazz musicians are heard in unusual settings and contexts; they are permitted a degree of musical freedom and opportunities for creativity not to be found in the normal course of night club and concert engagements."

The trouble is that sometimes no one bothers to tell the artists of this "main concern." Last year the late Jack Teagarden and Pee Wee Russell were to have been presented in a new context— straight mainstream improvisation rather than weary Dixieland routines. Despite the efforts of Gerry Mulligan to the contrary, the Russell-Teagarden ensemble performances turned into a kind of conventional Dixie hash, with slight swing-era overtones. Teagarden hadn't been told of the festival's plans for him.

This year clarinetist Russell returned, hoping to display his more modern side. He wound up playing the same tunes in essentially the same setting as last year. Even the introduction to his part of the show, sung by Jon Hendricks and Company, was identical to that of the year before. But no one seemed to care, except Russell. And pianist Dick Cary.

"Opportunities for creativity?" Cary, who is also a first rate composer with a modern workshop orchestra of his own in Los Angeles, arrived in Monterey last month with new and original music to be performed by a Russell "quartet." He then discovered the Russell company consisted of a large band of soloists, the same men with whom Cary had toured the Far East earlier in the year.

The Russell group fell back on its "safe" routine and Cary's portfolio was forgotten. When asked if he had discussed the problem with music consultant and programmer John Lewis, Cary said he had never even been introduced to Lewis.

Repeats from 1963, other than Russell, included the Modern Jazz Quartet, Miles Davis, Dizzy Gillespie, Thelonious Monk and Gerry

Mulligan. And Jon Hendricks, a charming entertainer but not a musician of sufficient stature to warrant appearances at Monterey over and over again.

For all the talent that resides in these fine musicians, Monterey badly needs new faces, new names and much more new music.

This year the only really new work came from Charles Mingus. It was like a therapeutic shock treatment, making some of us aware of how the festival had generally begun to fall into complacency, relative narrowness of outlook and even a "play it safe" posture. Those who cared also noticed that the customary Statement of Policy, the written guarantee of Monterey's superiority over other jazz festivals, was omitted from this season's printed program.

Any ambitious concert production involving many musicians and a large budget is bound to have some plans go sour. Monterey's ailment is not a matter of occasional musical misfires or clumsy programming. It's fundamentally a problem of musical myopia.

What is needed at Monterey is broader vision, rededication to original principles and a willingness to consistently reach beyond the familiar and comfortable. A child, however attractive, cannot remain a child; it must either grow up or ultimately expire.

San Francisco Examiner
October 4, 1964

Denny Zeitlin, 1966

Playing It Too Safe?

by Philip Elwood

In three weeks, on Sept. 15–16–17, the tenth Monterey Jazz Festival will again attract thousands of the jazz faithful to the most esthetically pleasing of concert sites, the Monterey County fairgrounds.

Unfortunately, the faithful of Monterey are often more devoted to the festivities than they are to the jazz; they have become less demanding, less discriminating and more loudly appreciative of the musical expressions on stage as the years have gone by at Monterey.

Although last year's festival was one of the least satisfying, and virtually no artists had been announced by the end of this year's season ticket sale (July 31), more than twice as many full-series tickets were purchased this year than for any previous festival.

From the moment that Dizzy Gillespie opened the first Monterey Jazz Festival in 1958 with an unaccompanied trumpet rendition of "The Star Spangled Banner," the event has presented some of the most unusual and exciting jazz expressions of its time.

In the early years of the MJF its most significant contribution to jazz came from the presentation of a broad cross-section of this expansive and vibrant music.

The oldest of blues and New Orleans styles were often matched over a typical Monterey weekend by some of the most provocative new sounds in jazz.

For instance, the weekend in 1960 that saw Jon Hendricks premiere his remarkable "Evolution of the Blues," a competent and entertaining history of vocal blues styles, Ornette Coleman and John Coltrane presented a joint Saturday afternoon concert which introduced their radical jazz sounds and musical attitudes to thousands of new listeners. And it was one of the best performances that either ever gave.

But the festival, it would seem, has gone soft and conservative recently. If the prospectus for 1967 indicates anything, this year the MJF has decided to play it safe by presenting almost exclusively tried-and-true established, and popular, performers.

This in spite of the Monterey Statement of Policy (paragraph five) which states, "Monterey introduces important unknown artists and reacquaints the public with neglected jazz giants, rather than 'play it safe' with a parade of name attractions" (sic).

The Monterey audience has become an older and increasingly square and unaware group. Whereas a whole new world of individual jazz expression has developed in the decade of Jazz Festival history, virtually none is noted for this year's fete. Ornette Coleman, who was signed only last week for a Sunday matinee performance, is the lone exception so far, and Ornette is an old liberal of jazz compared to the young radicals of the late 1960's.

Gil Melle's Electronic Jazz Quartet will also play Sunday afternoon. This is a group featuring specially made electronic instruments and an automated rostrum-podium which "conducts" by means of flashing cue-lights which are controlled by circuit cards fed into the machine.

Interesting stuff, but is it even close in its artistic merit to the strongly personal jazz expressions of such Monterey-neglected and important jazzmen as Cecil Taylor, Roland Kirk, Archie Shepp, the Don Friedman-Atilla Zoller groups, or many, many more who have been contributing to jazz in the clubs and on records for five years, yet have never been to Monterey? Or how about the New Orleans Preservation Hall band, or even Stan Kenton's fine current band?

Mel Torme, Dizzy Gillespie, Woody Herman, Earl Hines, Illinois Jacquet . . . the roster for Monterey this year, for the most part, reads like a 78 rpm top-bop record list of 20 years ago.

By including, again, a Saturday afternoon blues program, this time with B. B. King, T-Bone Walker, Muddy Waters, and others, the Monterey Festival is continuing an admirable tradition. But the blues are just a wellspring of jazz inspiration, just as they are the basis of rock'n'roll, which is acknowledged by the including of Big Brother and the Holding Company and the magnificent singer Janis Joplin.

And precisely as the finest rock groups are those who have created their own sounds from the blues, so has it always been the jazz instrumentalists who projected their inspired artistry above and beyond the blues form who became the international jazz giants.

Monterey has already had a Pop Festival this year; let's hope it isn't getting close to having another one.

Sunday San Francisco Examiner-Chronicle
August 27, 1967

It's That Time Again in Monterey

by John L. Wasserman

Well, it's Monterey Jazz Festival time again, kids, and maestro Jimmy Lyons has come up with a quintessential program to mark this 16th year of the oldest non-floating American jazz festival.

The essence of Monterey has long since become defined. It means theme shows, blues on Saturday afternoon, jazz kiddies on Sunday afternoon, the "surprise guests" so dear to Lyons's heart, some unexpected pleasures and a vast number of veteran, big-name mainstream jazz artists of unarguable worth, stature, and popularity.

Lyons and Monterey have years ago abandoned any pretense at presenting a full spectrum of jazz designed to appeal to all segments of the public. There have been occasional token musicians from the avant-garde but even these have been veterans with a stature of their own, i.e., an Ornette Coleman, who might be defined as mainstream experimental.

That's fine, too, unless you are advertising yourself as a showcase for tomorrow as well as yesterday. Lyons does not do this. He is quite frank. To him, Monterey is almost a child, his baby, and if you have a baby you like, you do not turn it in for a new model every year. The limbs of that baby are those musicians with whom Lyons has, in effect, grown up and with whom he has been friends for many years. Lyons is somewhere around 50; as is his musical director John Lewis; the Modern Jazz Quartet, bassist Ray Brown, pianist Ellis Larkins, guitarist Mundell Lowe, trumpet player Clark Terry, drummer Max Roach, singer Carmen McRae, alto saxophonist Sonny Stitt, trumpet player Thad Jones, singer Jon Hendricks and so on and on. Rhetorically, all are playing Monterey this weekend. Also unnecessary to say, all have played Monterey before. And likely will again.

With this booking philosophy has come tremendous success. Each year of recent times, the Festival played to around 90 percent capacity for the three-day, five-concert program. Lyons has developed and nurtured an audience for Monterey. They, in turn, know what they will get every year: good, solid music, nothing excessively jarring, a lot of fun, a lot of stars, a few surprises and, in many cases, smashed out of their melons.

Indeed, Monterey has become a party, both in Lyons's conception and in fact. It is a place for a weekend respite from everyday woes, for renewing annual friendships, for wearing funny hats and drinking cold beer and dancing in the aisles (usually to Big Joe Turner) and sitting up under the grandstand roof, chit-chatting the warm summer day away.

Monterey is not without its flaws. Aforementioned chit-chatters—well-fortified, of course—can create a quite remarkable din. And the predictability of many performers is not conducive to excitement. But to correct this would be to demand that Monterey be something it isn't and doesn't try to be. Given his stated and implied goals, Jimmy Lyons has created an event of flawless consistency.

San Francisco Chronicle
September 21, 1973

Ornette Coleman

Index

184